What people are saying about...

# A Whirlwind of Ash

"These are thoughtful reflections, filled with mind-catching imagery, which will make my personal celebration of Lent far richer this year. The reflection questions are often provocative or unsettling—as lenten prods should be. The use of Psalms each day serves to bring us back into the presence of a community at prayer. The great astonishment, as Father Juknialis underscores it, is that Lent is a time for God's work in us, even more than it is a time for our own human efforts. This is a study of God's grace, in bite-sized morsels, but big enough for a truly holy and sacred lenten lunch!"

† Richard J. Sklba
Auxiliary Bishop of Milwaukee

"Joe Juknialis has a gift for dipping into the human story we call 'Good News.' His ability to link 'Our Story' and 'The Story' enables readers to make further connections and spin-offs, and thus are excellent sources for prayer, reflection, and preaching. I have been helped much by this way of finding God in the ordinary, the Divine in the daily. This book is filled with wisdom and I highly recommend it."

Michael Crosby, OFM Cap.
Author, *Spirituality of the Beatitudes*

"In a sea of lenten books, this one stands out for its remarkable clarity, consistency of theme, and imagination. The title *A Whirlwind of Ash* draws together the traditional symbol of ashes with the fresh image of a whirlwind that changes, stirs, moves, and rearranges everything in an instant. Both images forcibly set the season in focus: change is as vital to life as spring, and change is wrought first and foremost by God in our lives. These meditations are thought-provoking, and by turns prophetic, lyric, rueful, and comforting. They intend to make us more human, more humble, more forgiving, and more daring by the time Lent culminates in Holy Week. This is a soul-searching book."

Megan McKenna
Author, *Reflections on Advent, Christmas, and Epiphany*

"Do you seek a deeper appreciation of your lenten journey? Look no further. You'll find it in *A Whirlwind of Ash: Daily Reflections and Psalm Prayers*. Juknialis' ability to discover God's hand at work in our everyday experiences is matched by his imaginative, poetic way of expressing this discovery. If I were allowed to recommend only one book of reflections for the lenten journey I wouldn't hesitate to recommend this one."

Rev. Andre Papineau, SDS
Associate Professor of Pastoral Studies
Sacred Heart School of Theology
Hales Corners, WI

"The season of Lent is the time of the church's annual retreat. During it, we are invited to step back and reflect on the mystery of salvation, not merely for the sake of understanding the historical events themselves, but in order to examine our lives through the lens of these events. With this book, Joseph Juknialis provides us with a way of doing just this. The liturgical readings of the season are the springboard for these reflections, which are grounded in contemporary life experience. In this way they open the readings to new understandings, and they open our lives to the religious treasures of Lent."

Dianne Bergant, C.S.A., Ph.D.
Professor of Biblical Studies
Catholic Theological Union in Chicago

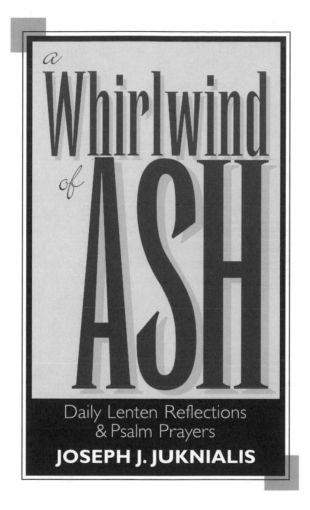

# a Whirlwind of ASH

Daily Lenten Reflections
& Psalm Prayers

**JOSEPH J. JUKNIALIS**

XXIII

TWENTY-THIRD PUBLICATIONS

Mystic, CT 06355

# Dedication

To the Catholic faith communities of
St. James in Menomonee Falls, Wisconsin, and
SS. Peter and Paul in Milwaukee, Wisconsin.
Their faith called forth these reflections
on life and the Gospel.

Other books by Joseph J. Juknialis:
  *Winter Dreams and other such friendly dragons*
  *When God Began in the Middle*
  *Angels to Wish By*
  *A Stillness without Shadows*
  *Stories for Christian Initiation*
  *Crushed into Glory*
  *Deepdown Spirituality*
All are published by Resource Publications, San Jose, CA.

The psalm passages contained herein are from the *New Revised Standard Version of the Bible*, © 1989, by the Division of Christian Education of the National Council of Churches of Christ in the U.S.A. Used by permission. All rights reserved.

Twenty-Third Publications
185 Willow Street
P.O. Box 180
Mystic, CT 06355
(860) 536-2611
(800) 321-0411

ISBN 0-89622-963-7
Library of Congress Catalog Card Number 98-75052
Printed in the U.S.A.

# Table of Contents

Introduction ..............................1

Week of Ash Wednesday ..............4

First Week of Lent.....................13

Second Week of Lent.................29

Third Week of Lent ...................45

Fourth Week of Lent .................65

Fifth Week of Lent....................85

Passion Sunday .......................106

Holy Thursday.........................114

Good Friday ...........................116

Easter Vigil ............................118

# A Whirlwind of Ash

# ·⌒· Introduction

"Remember that you are dust, and unto dust you shall return." Like the twelfth stroke at midnight of a new year's eve, the words usher in a new time: lenten time. Like sitting on our father's shoulders, Lent offers a chance to look behind and see from where we have come, only now with a bit of a wince as we recognize our own sin among those past shadows. With an uncomfortable awe, we turn and gaze upon an uncertain future as we are carried forward.

Much of each lenten season calls us to conversion, to change both our ways and our hearts. It seems to me, however, that few of us ever do much changing. It is not that we don't want to change, or even that we don't try. It is that most of us are pretty much incapable of bringing ourselves to embrace the radical life shifts that change initiates. We may eat less during Lent, or give up smoking or drinking, or pray more, but mostly we go back to our old ways once Resurrection-time comes. In fact we usually can't wait for Easter to arrive so we can return to the life-styles we truly enjoy.

Oh, there may be those times, once or twice in a lifetime if at all, when a radical change does take place, but they are hardly our doing. They come imposed upon us from the outside, times when we are forced to face our addiction or a collapsing marriage or a life-threatening illness or the dwindling energies that accompany growing older. At such times either we change or our worlds die, so we give in and grudgingly go along with the forces of life. No, we don't choose to change. Life seems to change us.

Curiously, much of the new life which arises in our lives and in our spirits comes from what has changed without our ever having done anything, from the remnants of burned-out loves and dimmed dreams and ashen memories of failure. Change does seem to take place in our lives, but only because something has first collapsed. Then from those ashes the phoenix rises. The fact is that such transformation is taking place constantly, within us and about us, like a whirlwind. We are being made new, yet mostly it happens without our recognizing it.

It is the premise of this book that what we are experiencing are the actions of our God. It is not we who change ourselves or one another. It is God who changes us. Thus this collection of lenten reflections is intended to be an invitation to reflect, over the course of forty days, on what it is that God has been doing in our lives.

1

In that light, this book looks not to the future but to the past, for that is where God has been active in our lives. It is not the purpose of this book to invite you or challenge you to change, simply because that is God's doing. The purpose of this book is not to get you to do anything except, perhaps, to recognize what it is that God has already done in you. Then, both you and I might be moved to allow God to do even more.

Many folks seem to be captured by the image of the prophet Elijah standing at the entrance to a cave carved in the side of Mount Horeb (1 Kings 19). As the story tells, God was not in the mighty wind passing by or in the earthquake or in the fire but in the still small voice, the whispering sound. There is something intriguing here about the gentleness of God's power.

Nevertheless, God also comes as a strong and driving wind, a whirlwind, in fact, from which nothing can escape—especially the ashes of our lives. It is that God who once came with a strong easterly wind to turn the sea into dry land so that the Hebrews might pass and be freed from the slavery of Egypt (Exodus 14). It is that same God who came in a whirlwind to take the prophet Elijah into heaven (2 Kings 2). This is the God who sorts the innocent from the guilty by whirlwind and storm (Nahum 1). And it is God's Spirit that came as a mighty wind, filling houses and Pentecost lives (Acts 2).

God is a whirlwind moving through our lives in such a way that nothing can withstand that holy power. All is caught up into it, even the leftover ash of our lives. In the end, it is not we who change ourselves but always our God who changes us. What Lent invites us to do is to recognize that holy whirlwind of ash.


*Note:* There is only one reflection for the First Sunday in Lent, the Second Sunday in Lent, and Passion Sunday (the other Sundays have a separate reflection for each of the three cycles). Since the themes for the first two Sundays and Passion Sunday are so similar, I decided that one reflection would be sufficient for all three cycles.

# Ash
# Wednesday

# ·⟋⁀· Ash Wednesday

Joel 2:12–18; 2 Corinthians 5:20—6:2; Matthew 6:1–6, 16–18

*Whenever you give alms, do not sound a trumpet before you…*
*whenever you pray, do not stand and pray at street corners…*
*whenever you fast, do not look dismal.*

A recent issue of *U.S. News & World Report* featured an article on the business of pornography. It has become respectable, they observed, or at least culturally acceptable. The article noted that the pornography industry distributed $75 million worth of hardcore videos in 1985; ten years later the video market had grown to $665 million. So who are the people who buy these videos?

In one way or another, I suppose, they are believers and non-believers alike. So they are we, simply because believers are both sinners and non-sinners on any list of sinfulness we might choose to post. We find ourselves cheerleading capital punishment despite Jesus' call for compassion. We hoard our goods even though Jesus lived simply. We paint our lives with revenge even though Jesus forgave. And so the list goes on.

The point is that in all of us there is a life beneath our life, an "us" beneath our us. There is a backyard behind our frontyard, a nighttime me as well as a daytime me. In fact, at times our backyard is so deep, so lost in darkness, that we can live without ever having explored it— yet it is there. In George Bernanos's *The Diary of a Country Priest*, the priest says it yet another way:

> I believe, in fact I am certain, that many of us never give out the whole of ourselves, our deepest truth. We live on the surface, and yet, so rich is the soil of humanity that even this thin outer layer is able to yield a kind of meager harvest which gives the illusion of real living.

That is what Lent is about, at least I think what a good piece of it should be about. It is a chance to give out a bit more of ourselves, if to no one else at least then to our own self-denying selves. Thus, in some way or another, we might come to know a bit more clearly who we really are, persons of sinfulness as well as of virtue.

Christian tradition has offered us three ways of coming to that state of self-knowledge. Lent is a good time to come back to them.

*Prayer.* Maybe better than the talking-to-God type of prayer might be the God-talking to us type of prayer, which is to suggest that one simply sits with the silence. For ten minutes at a time over forty days or forty nights, who-knows-what begins to come to the surface just because we let God do it. We begin to see what we did not know was there or did not want to know was there. It becomes a shard of light escaping out of our darkness.

*Almsgiving.* This reminds us that there is a whole world out there in need of our caring. Almsgiving not only brings that world into the light but also prods us to see our own quiet indifference.

*Fasting.* It is hard to give up something for a lengthy time and not come to realize how hooked we have become on it. So then, what is really prime in our lives? What is frontstage and center—or perhaps backstage but directing the whole show? More than hunger pangs can be felt when we are fasting, especially if we are willing to sit in the silence and think about it.

*The pieces of our lives which lie beneath the surface often edge themselves, slowly, into consciousness. Over time we begin to say, "Someday I've got to do something about that." What is lying beneath the surface of your life that needs to come into the light?*

## Prayer • psalm 51

R. Be merciful, O Lord, for we have sinned.

Have mercy on me, O God,
according to your steadfast love;
according to your abundant mercy
blot out my transgressions. R.

Create in me a clean heart, O God,
and put a new and right spirit within me.
do not cast me away from your presence,
and do not take your holy spirit from me. R.

Restore to me the joy of your salvation,
and sustain in me a willing spirit.
O Lord, open my lips,
and my mouth will declare your praise. R.

# ᏒᏒ Thursday after Ash Wednesday

Deuteronomy 30:15–20; Luke 9:22–25

*I have set before you life and death, blessings and curses.*
*Choose life so that you may live.*

Much of life is imposed upon us; there is much we do not choose—the premature death of someone we love, lifelong illness, divorce, addictions, job loss, unsettling colleagues, even some of our own personality traits. In so many notable ways, life seems to choose us rather than the other way around. And frequently, it does not seem very fair.

On the other hand, there are those portions of our lives that we do seem to have at least some control over—whom we marry, the job or profession which occupies much of our waking time, where we decide to live, how we spend our money. Such things we choose for ourselves, and these choices give us a sense of control, or at least a tit-for-tat sense of balance to counteract the unpredictable and the imposed.

There is another aspect of who we are which we are able to choose as well—not that we always do, however, but we do have that freedom. We can choose if we want to be compassionate or not, if we want to be forgiving or vengeful, generous or greedy, gentle or demanding. We can decide to become patient or understanding or honest or caring for the weak among us. Such choices pretty much stand before us for most of our lives—always present, always reversible.

What we also come to realize over time is that those aspects of who we are which we choose do impact those aspects of our lives which we do not choose. In other words, whether or not we are compassionate or merciful or generous affects how we deal with the tragedies of death and illness and life changes. Positive choices regarding patience and honesty and the like do not necessarily eliminate the tragic, but do affect the way we respond to them and how they impact our day-to-day living. Slowly through life we come to realize that.

So Lent comes somewhat as a retreat of forty days and forty nights, a time to look once more at some of our life choices and to decide where we want to stand and who it is we want to be. And we do so realizing that often enough what seems to be life-giving can be deadly, like having our own way all the time, for example. And sometimes what seems to be deadly is indeed life giving, like loving even when it hurts.

Each year, then, we take these five or six weeks out of the year to look at the life set before us. Each year we quietly and as honestly as we can consider who we are and who it is we are becoming. Each year we find before us both life and death, and each year we recommit ourselves to choosing life as best we can by loving the Lord, our God, by heeding his voice, and by holding fast to him.

*Consider your life. Consider who you are and who you want to be. Which portions of yourself do you want to hold on to? Which are worth keeping? Which portions could use some reshaping?*

## Prayer • psalm 1

R. Happy are they who hope in the Lord.

Happy are those who do not follow
the advice of the wicked,
or take the path that sinners tread,
or sit in the seat of scoffers;
but their delight is in the law of the Lord,
and on his law they meditate day and night. R.

They are like trees planted by streams of water,
which yield their fruit in its seasons,
and their leaves do not wither.
In all that they do, they prosper. R.

The wicked are not so,
but are like chaff that the wind drives away.
The Lord watches over the way of the righteous,
but the way of the wicked will perish. R.

# Friday after Ash Wednesday

Isaiah 58:1–9; Matthew 9:14–15

*Is not this the fast that I choose…to share your bread with
the hungry, and bring the homeless poor into your house?*

Life has a way of getting backwards so that we are not quite sure
which way was meant to be frontwards. Take college students, for
example. They and not the faculty are supposed to be the liberal and
radical species on a college campus. These days, however, it seems to
be the other way around. It is the faculty that seems to be out front.
Not that they are marching on picket lines; but they are the ones
prodding students into stretching the limits of current thinking. The
students are certainly not in need of being held back.

Government and citizenry may be yet another instance. We have
come to expect government to be flawed, certainly not to be the beacon of moral uprightness or the prophet for cultural and societal ren-
ovation. One would expect the citizenry to be the moral watchdog of
government, insuring that elected officials are not siphoning off the
gravy leaving nothing but leftover grease for the people. These are
days of inverted weather, however, when strange and unexpected
winds blow across the landscape.

Sometime back when the national mood sought to cut care for
newcomers in our land, it was the assembled governors of our nation
who called for greater attention to the legal immigrants, for increased
revenue to care for their needs. At other times it has been the execu-
tive branch of the national government that has sought extended
health care for those helplessly and hopelessly afflicted but without
any resources. It has been government, also, that has warned against
inclinations toward isolationism and that has exposed our racial
drifts back into prejudice and intolerance. Somehow it seems that big
government has at times become our moral compass. Could it be the
spirit of Isaiah is still alive?

It was the poet Isaiah who turned the notion of fasting inside out.
Instead of less (as in food), he challenged for more (as in more freedom for the oppressed and more bread for the hungry and more shel-
ters for the homeless and more attention to the needs of one's weaker citizenry). So fasting as giving up became fasting as giving out—
one more confusing turn around which has become the Christian

norm for living as Jesus did.

It is also why Jesus did not seem concerned about his followers not doing any fasting—of the giving up kind. Jesus had picked up on Isaian fasting—the giving out kind—and did it himself. Then he suggested that when he was gone, it would be the time for his disciples and you and me and everyone else to follow suit. Then would be the time to fast—to give out—because a new world was being ushered in, one in which God reigns and gives out to *all* the people.

*How do you fast? What expectations do you have of fasting? If you do not fast at all, why not?*

## Prayer • psalm 51

R. A broken, humbled heart, O God, you will not scorn.

Have mercy on me, O God,
according to your steadfast love;
according to your abundant mercy
blot out my transgressions.
Wash me thoroughly from my iniquity,
and cleanse me from my sin. R.

For I know my transgressions,
and my sin is ever before me.
Against you, you alone, have I sinned,
and done what is evil in your sight. R.

For you have no delight in sacrifice;
if I were to give a burnt offering,
you would not be pleased.
The sacrifice acceptable to God is a broken spirit;
a broken and contrite heart, O God,
you will not despise. R.

# ⌒ Saturday after Ash Wednesday

Isaiah 58:9–14; Luke 5:27–32

*Jesus saw a tax collector named Levi, and said to him, "Follow me."*
*And he got up, left everything, and followed him.*

We like to pride ourselves on being free—not just because we are Americans (who sense we somehow created the market on freedom), but also and more basically because we are human beings. We do not hesitate to point out how we live immersed in a candyland of sweet choices (or at least our consumer psyche doesn't hesitate). And so, of course, we deem ourselves free.

For breakfast we can choose among pop-tarts or corn flakes or toast and jelly or bacon and eggs. And so, of course, we are free. We are able to choose what car to drive—a Geo or an Explorer, a Caravan or a Lexus. We can wear our hair long or short, natural or dyed, curled or wavy or straight. And so, of course, we are free—because we can choose.

We like to think there are no limits. But of course there are. The fact is, so often the more significant the choice, the more fragile the freedom we fantasize. We think we can be with our lives whatever we want to be. Yet the truth is that our freedoms are limited—by academic ability or native skills (someone 5'10" tall and 140 pounds is unlikely to ever play pro basketball). We are limited by age (sixty-year-old hard rock stars tend not to draw big crowds). We are limited by what the market will bear (our country does not need more than one president or our city more than one mayor). So in some ways we are not so free to choose.

Nor are we free to choose to marry whom we wish. Marriage is always a mutual decision, and more than one passionate love has wallowed in failure when the beloved did not respond. We are not always free to choose, or to say it yet another way—our choices are not always the same choices others make.

We are, however, free to choose our life-style—our value system, what or who shapes our dreams and the texture of our response to life. We can choose between loving care and indifference, between forgiveness and retribution, between generosity and a hoarding spirit, between patience and our own self-will. And, in the process of a lifetime and based upon those choices, you and I find ourselves

10

increasingly or decreasingly becoming a follower of the Lord Jesus—
sometimes consciously and sometimes not so consciously.

The fruit born of graced choices, we slowly come to realize, is not
a life lived calmly and without any storminess, but rather a life of
deepening peace. In the end we find ourselves with more joy, less
gloom, and renewed in a strength which sustains. And that takes
place no matter what else happens, regardless of who we gather at
table with, no matter where life's journey may map our steps. Those
who follow the Lord Jesus sense, then, that they are riding the heights
of what it means to be human.

*Look over the span of your life. Note whether your joy and strength
and peace are growing or decreasing. How are you becoming more
human or less human? by choice or by coincidence?*

## Prayer • psalm 86

R. Teach me your way, O Lord.

Incline your ear, O Lord, and answer me,
for I am poor and needy.
Preserve my life, for I am devoted to you;
save your servant who trusts in you. R.

You are my God; be gracious to me, O Lord,
for to you do I cry all day long.
Gladden the soul of your servant,
for to you, O Lord, I lift up my soul. R.

For you, O Lord, are good and forgiving,
abounding in steadfast love to all who call on you.
Give ear, O Lord, to my prayer;
listen to my cry of supplication. R.

# The First Week of Lent

# ⋏⋅ The First Sunday

Year A: Genesis 2:7–9; 3:1–7; Romans 5:12–19, Matthew 4:1–11
Year B: Genesis 9:8–15, 1 Peter 3:18–22, Mark 1:12–15
Year C: Deuteronomy 26:4–10, Romans 10:8–13, Luke 4:1–13

*I have set my bow in the clouds, and it shall be a sign*
*of the covenant between me and the earth.*

I went back to the old neighborhood a while ago, back to Sheboygan, Wisconsin, where I had spent the first eight years of my life. I realized there what everyone who has ever tried to go home discovers: that the trees have grown smaller and easier for climbing, that the alley where we played hide-and-go-seek has grown narrower, the trip to the corner less daring, and all the old haunts so much less intriguing.

But going back also drew forth in me a power I had not imagined or expected. Not only did it reintroduce me to who I am, it renewed the dream of who I could be. Going back to one's roots can do that because it is a going back to where it all began.

Sometimes nostalgia gets a bad rap for being too much cotton candy, for living on borrowed dreams whose return date is long overdue. Maybe so, in part at least. But nostalgia can also be that means by which we remember what we once held onto as true, back to a future not yet polluted by our sin, back to a time when everything was possible because no one had yet slammed any doors shut—not even the one of holiness. And once back there we have the option of reclaiming it for the present. It's good to go back to one's roots.

Lent can be such a time, of returning to our roots. Some would see the season as penitential, a time of reparation for sin. Others see it as a time for growing more prayerful or for reestablishing lives of service or for deepening faith. And it can be all of that. Yet the readings of this lenten Sunday—the first of this "joyful season," as one of the lenten prefaces refers to it—take us back to how it once was and who was once doing the shaping of life.

Throughout the readings of this First Sunday of Lent, in any of the cycles, the Scriptures take us back in time. The gospel story especially is one of Jesus drawn by God's Spirit into the desert and tempted there with all sorts of hungers and pangs and visions. Yet each time he returns to the Scriptures that root his faith and his response. So, then, the invitation comes for us to live life with the memory of how it once was in order that this memory might be our strength and our light.

There are myriad ways of making the lenten journey back to our roots. Spend time with the Scriptures. Read the lives of the saints. Go on a retreat. Visit a shrine. Keep a journal. Pray the rosary again. Sit with silence. Make the stations of the cross. Offer peace to an enemy. Visit the sick or a shut-in. Give enough alms to notice the pinch. Do some spiritual reading. Fast and abstain from meat. They are all part of our tradition and shards of our own pasts. In them we will once more meet ourselves perhaps as if for the first time and remember dreams long lost in the clutter of life's demands.

There is a caution, however. If we seek to make a journey back to our roots and not simply into nostalgia, we need to remember that roots, if they are healthy and alive, are always found in the dirt and the mud. A journey back to our roots, then, will also place us square in the midst of all of our life's unattractive earthiness. But then the word "lent" means springtime so it should not surprise us that new shoots will spring forth from our roots and all of that in which they are embedded.

*Name a dream which you once had for yourself—a dream for your spirit, of who you could become—that has since faded. What sort of lenten practice might bring you back to the roots of that dream?*

## ✝ Prayer • psalm 25

R. Your ways, O Lord, are love and truth,
to those who keep your covenant.

Make me to know your ways, O Lord;
teach me your paths.
Lead me in your truth, and teach me,
for you are the God of my salvation. R.

Be mindful of your mercy, O Lord,
and of your steadfast love,
for they have been from of old.
Do not remember the sins of my youth
or my transgressions. R.

Good and upright is the Lord;
therefore he instructs sinners in the way.
He leads the humble in what is right,
and teaches the humble his way. R.

# ·⌒· Monday, the First Week

Leviticus 19:1–2,11–18; Matthew 25:31–46

*And the king will answer them, "Truly I tell you, just as you did it to one of the least of these brothers and sisters of mine, you did it to me."*

In his book *Philemon's Problem: the Daily Dilemma of the Christian*, James Burtchaell tells the story of Pinocchio the puppet. He offers it as a metaphor for understanding our sin and our blindness to it all. It is a most poignant tale for our human condition.

As the story unfolds, there was a time when Pinocchio was a most troublesome puppet, very much in need of changing his ways by a strong dose of love and compassion to replace his wooden heart. With the hope of such a conversion, arrangements were made for him to tour the confines of hell so that perhaps with a portion of what we would today call reality therapy, he might repent.

Having arrived at the fiery depths, he began to take inventory of the people there, of those who in their lives on earth had failed the test. Not far from where he stood he saw a beautiful ballerina, dancing and spinning with much grace. As he approached her, she danced a marvelous pirouette and spun right past him without even taking note of his presence. Not far away he could see a carpenter at work, and so Pinocchio made his way there to talk with him. But the carpenter was so engrossed with his work, sawing and hammering and measuring, that he too was never aware of the wooden puppet at his side.

From there Pinocchio made his way to the next person, and the next, and the next, and so it went. And what Pinocchio eventually came to realize was that in hell everyone was so captivated by themselves and what they were about that each was oblivious to anyone else. Indeed, there was no love there just as there was none among so many on earth. At that point, Pinocchio realized the errors of his ways and returned home a repentant puppet.

In many ways, I suppose, the story of Pinocchio is also our own story. And what strikes me as a bit sad about it all, and also more than a bit fearful, is that each of us seldom knows how blind we are to everyone but ourselves. How do I or you or any of us know we have a plank in our eye that keeps us from even recognizing a speck of someone else's need?

In Matthew's last judgment scene the sheep were separated from the goats based upon whether or not they fed their neighbor, or clothed them, or visited them, or cared for them. But that judgment took place regardless of whether or not they realized the eternal significance of it all, regardless of whether they knew they should. "Lord, when was it that we saw you hungry or thirsty or a stranger or naked or sick or in prison, and did not take care of you?" Having been blind to the human situation and its significance matters not at all. We cannot say, "But I didn't know."

Perhaps Lent is about learning to see again; if not that then at least about *asking* the Lord that we might see once more—or in some instances, for the first time. If we cannot see the plank in our own eye, then we cannot possibly know we are blind. Maybe by some curious twist of logic you and I must simply presume that we are in one way or another blind. And the only way out is for the Lord to be our light, for if he is not then there can be no seeing whatsoever. Lent, then, is not about what we do but more about what we decide to let the Lord do—which is to enable us to see.

*What is it that you now see at this point in your life that you did not see ten or twenty years ago? Spend some time in prayer asking the Lord to remove any blindness you may have.*

## ⟋• Prayer • psalm 19

R. Your words, Lord, are spirit and life.

The law of the Lord is perfect,
reviving the soul;
the decrees of the Lord are sure,
making wise the simple. R.

The precepts of the Lord are right,
rejoicing the heart;
the commandment of the Lord is clear,
enlightening the eyes. R.

Let the words of my mouth
and the meditation of my heart
be acceptable to you,
O Lord, my rock and my redeemer. R.

# ◝ Tuesday, the First Week

Isaiah 55:10–11; Matthew 6:7–15

*Your father knows what you need before you ask him.*

Prayer. Why do we keep asking? If God knows what we need better than we know what we need ("Your Father knows what you need before you ask him"), why do we keep asking? If our prayer is not a way of twisting God's arm until God cries "uncle" and gives in ("They think they will win a hearing by the sheer multiplication of words"), why do we keep asking?

It may be that we cannot believe God really loves us all that much, loves us more than we love ourselves. It may be that we who feel so unlovable and unloving just cannot imagine a God so generous. However, it may also be our helplessness. It may be those moments when we "hit the wall," when we who have tried everything are finally forced to our knees and admit we can't do it by ourselves. And so we look to God simply because we have nowhere else to look. It is then that we become believers.

Oftentimes those who do not go to God with much frequency during the good times feel guilty about going to God when they are in trouble. It is as if to say, "I do not really care about God. I just use God when I need God." So for them it becomes a feeling of awkwardness. Yet in the end, they and we crouch behind our guilt and go to God anyway simply because we do not know what else to do.

It may just be that such a response is okay with our God. After all, God has always been a God of the poor, and that is part of what being poor means—being helpless. The other part is being dependent. So we go on bended knee, or even on straight knees if that is more convenient or less obvious, just because we do not know what else to do. At such times our asking is not so much arm-twisting as it is a last resort plea made with reckless abandon. It is not so much refusing to believe God loves us enough as believing that God loves us so much that we can go even when we are not deserving.

Most of the time, though, we never think it through that way. Maybe none of the time. We just do it; and that's okay. It is the way we become believers—coming to know there must be a God because good things came forth when, out of all of our own personal chaos, we didn't even know what good to ask for. It is precisely at such moments of crunched and squished history that we find ourselves

18

saying "holy be your name, because it sure can't be in my name that all this happened," and "your will be done on earth, because I can't even put words to what I think my will might be." That is when real conversion takes place. That is when Lent really happens, this time of year or any time of year.

*Why do you pray? What do you believe about the relationship between praying and its outcome? Which phrase of the Our Father best describes your life at this time? Which phrase would currently make a good title for your biography?*

## Prayer • psalm 34

R. From all their afflictions God will deliver the just.

O magnify the Lord with me,
and let us exalt his name together.
I sought the Lord, and he answered me,
and delivered me from all my fears. R.

Look to him, and be radiant;
so your faces shall never be ashamed.
This poor soul cried, and was heard by the Lord,
and was saved from every trouble. R.

The eyes of the Lord are on the righteous,
and his ears are open to their cry.
The face of the Lord is against evildoers,
to cut off the remembrance of them from the earth. R.

When the righteous cry for help, the Lord hears,
and rescues them from all their troubles.
The Lord is near to the brokenhearted,
and saves the crushed in spirit. R

# ⌒· Wednesday, the First Week

Jonah 3:1–10; Luke 11:29–32

*For just as Jonah became a sign to the people of Nineveh,*
*so the Son of Man will be to this generation.*

You really had to be there, and those who were are slowly passing away, at least according to a *Newsweek* magazine tally (February 24, 1997). The author offered a sampling of when the last witnesses to the twentieth century's most memorable events will pass from the scene. The estimated year of death for the last witnesses to several notable events were:

Chicago Cubs win the World Series......................year 2013
World War I veterans ..............................................year 2005
1929 stock market crash..........................................year 2035
John F. Kennedy's assassination ............................year 2074
O.J. Simpson criminal trial ....................................year 2108

Something will be lost in the passing of those who witnessed those events. A sense of continuity. Some wisdom, maybe. An awareness of the larger picture. Nevertheless, it will happen. Always has; always will.

Through it all the wisdom of Jesus endures, or else it stands in judgment upon us. Other events and their impact wane. As much as Jonah became the sign for the Ninevites and Solomon for the world of his day, we hold the Christ-event as the norm for making sense out of our life, the ultimate pattern for whittling our way through and around the knots and burls in our wood.

These days we find ourselves looking for quick and simple solutions to the problems and difficulties of life. Unwanted pregnancies can be quickly dismissed by abortion; unwanted illness and death by suicide. Unwanted individuals of society are eliminated by capital punishment; unwanted governments by bombs.

It is the wisdom of Jesus, however, that cautions how life is always messy and troublesome and never a quick negotiation. So we find ourselves going back to his standard, that of compassion and justice and mercy and generosity and trust and love. In the process we come to discover that it works. His way brings success to our living, if one is willing to view success through the lens of dying. Yet over the centuries believers have come to be believers simply because they and we have come to realize that the messiness and complexity of day-to-day living can only be lived by his wisdom, or we are never really able to live it at all.

I do not know that many of us do it very well. That's why there is reconciliation. Yet here at the beginning of this Lent we place ourselves once again under his standard—maybe with a bit of fear, sometimes out of a sense of obligation, but mostly because it works. And it works better than anything else we try. The lasting impact of the stock market crash will dwindle. What we have learned from World War I will be forgotten, and as a nation we will probably be condemned to repeat it. But we who are believers stand by Jesus and his wisdom as best we can.

*Which of Jesus' qualities is most difficult for you to live out? Do any come easily, almost second nature? If you could assure that one quality of Jesus be passed on to the next generation, which would it be? Which Christlike qualities are we as a society most in need of today?*

## ⟡ Prayer • psalm 51

R. A broken, humbled heart, O God, you will not scorn.

Have mercy on me, O God,
according to your steadfast love;
according to your abundant mercy
blot out my transgressions.
Wash me thoroughly from my iniquity,
and cleanse me from my sin. R.

Create in me a clean heart, O God,
and put a new and steadfast spirit within me.
Do not cast me away from your presence,
and do not take your holy spirit from me. R.

For you have no delight in sacrifice;
if I were to give a burnt offering, you would not be pleased.
The sacrifice acceptable to God is a broken spirit;
a broken and contrite heart, O God,
you will not despise. R.

# ✐ Thursday, the First Week

Esther 12:14–16, 23–25; Matthew 7:7–12

*If you, then, who are evil, know how to give good gifts*
*to your children, how much more will your Father in heaven*
*give good things to those who ask him!*

I'm not sure if the inclination to extravagance is a characteristic of infatuation or of love. Maybe both. I have been delightfully seduced by the generosity of infatuation, as I suspect we all have, and undoubtedly we have known enough love to know its magnanimity.

My grandparents spoiled me whenever I came to visit, and they did so in such a fashion that none of us were ever obligated by it. Such was their love. My grandmother would cook my favorite meals and let me eat in the living room while watching television and let me climb their apple trees and play along the railroad tracks where everyone in the neighborhood hung out—none of which I could ever do when I was with my parents. My grandparents were certainly extravagant with their love, it seemed to me.

And in my adult life I've been blessed as well with good friends—women and men who continue to amaze me by their generosity, not necessarily with their gifts (though at times that, too) but even more so by the many ways they leave the footsteps of their presence in my life. Human beings are indeed eager to bless.

If such is true with us who so often love so poorly, would it not be even more true with our God who is love, and is so extravagantly? Our God keeps reminding us of this, eager to give whenever asked, longing to open if we but seek, promising to unlock whenever we knock.

Nevertheless we wince, tempted to find the promise suspect, perhaps because we have all gone searching in fields of the divine only to come up empty-handed. We have prayed for healing and have grown weaker. We have asked for a job and found ourselves penniless. We have sought peace for our checkered families only to taste more of the alienation. We have even thought ourselves content if only the sun would shine on our picnic, then found ourselves huddled beneath umbrellas. Little wonder, then, that we have grown skeptical of the promise to hear our prayers with any sort of response, much less extravagance.

I suspect our God, however, is more a God of our spirits than of our weather or our economics. What we ultimately long for in a job is security, or peace from worry. Our prayer for healing is only a slice of our deeper desire for life, a long life lived fully. Our hunger for family unity is in truth a hunger for love. Even our umbrella problems are a simple hope that our planned picnic might be a doorway into tasting the joy we seek among family and friends. So then our prayers for the most part are but a whisper of our deepest desires such as love and joy and peace and life—namely, God.

Though at first it does not seem like God, in the end it is God we long for. It is in moments of faith that we have bumped into quiet peace, and into love and joy and all such other gifts as well. It is then that we have bumped into our God, more often unexpectedly and undeservedly. But then, that is how it so often seems with generosity and extravagance. And if we find it then without even asking, what might we discover if we dare to take the first step of such a life journey into faith by asking? Perhaps that is what the promise is all about—to expect not so much jobs or sunshine but the fullness of it all, the love and joy and peace that our God is.

*What do you expect from your prayer? What is it you get? What are the deepest desires rooted in your prayer? Have you ever been disappointed in the answers—or lack of—to your prayer?*

## ⌐• Prayer • psalm 138

R. Lord, on the day I called for help, you answered me.

I give you thanks, O Lord, with my whole heart;
before the gods I sing your praise;
I bow down toward your holy temple
and give thanks to your name
for your steadfast love and your faithfulness. R.

For you have exalted your name
and your word above everything.
On the day I called, you answered me,
you increased my strength of soul. R.

You stretch out your hand, and your right hand delivers me.
The Lord will fulfill his purpose for me;
your steadfast love, O Lord, endures forever.
Do not forsake the work of your hands. R.

# 〽️ Friday, the First Week

Ezekiel 18:21–28; Matthew 5:20–26

*So when you are offering your gift at the altar, first be reconciled to*
*your brother or sister, and then come and offer your gift.*

Tony told it with a smile, but also with a bit of a wince; and he read-
ily admitted as much. Twenty-five years ago he had been cut off by
another driver at the corner of Hampton and Teutonia Avenues. There
was no accident, just a lot of leftover anger. Neither driver knew each
other; neither stopped. It was simply a close call, nothing more. All
that remains of the incident today is Tony's anger, and it surfaces
every time he drives through that intersection, he says. As he spoke of
it, he wondered if in part his continual anger was not also an inabil-
ity to forgive that anonymous driver. If he could forgive, he reasoned,
maybe he would be freed of the anger as well.

Forgiveness is never easy for any of us. It is such a "tangled web we
weave"—reality and suspicion and imagination, hurt and anger and
feelings and thoughts and culpability. So when the issue of forgiveness arises, well, we are never quite sure what else is woven into the
snare. And we do not like moving on the issue lest we do or say more
than we ever intended. All of which does not solve the problem, and
so we sit with our anger.

All of this may be why Jesus insisted we do something when we
recognize that someone has something against us. His advice is to set
aside our gifts of bread (both the bread of our hands and the bread
of our lives), first go and be reconciled, and then come back to the
bread we were carrying. In other words, Jesus seems to suggest that
forgiveness is a matter of doing and not one of feeling.

Forgiveness, then, is not a question of emotions—of whether we
want to or whether we are ready to. Rather, forgiveness is doing,
choosing to build or rebuild in spite of our feelings. It is the courage
to do what must be done simply because it is what must be done,
regardless of the fact that most of us find ourselves wanting to run in
the opposite direction, never looking back. That is why forgiveness is
so difficult and why we so seldom do it well. Most of the time it takes
a great deal of courage, and most of the time we feel like the shaggy
lion in the story of the Wizard of Oz—more shaggy than courageous.

The truth is that forgiveness is something we do for ourselves and not for the other person. When we forgive, it is we who are made new; it is we who are freed; it is we who are given a future. That is why forgiveness is a good lenten journey, because Lent is about being made new and about finding our future once more. So this Lent, do yourself a favor and forgive someone. Pray for them. Send them some flowers, or maybe just a card. Write them a letter. Smile at them. Say something good about them to someone. Free yourself.

*Is there someone whom you need to forgive? Is there an event which you need to let go? For you, what is the most difficult part of forgiving someone?*

## Prayer • psalm 130

R. If you, O Lord, laid bare our guilt,
who could endure it?

Out of the depths I cry to you, O Lord.
Lord, hear my voice!
Let your ears be attentive
to the voice of my supplications! R.

If you, O Lord, should mark iniquities,
Lord, who could stand?
But there is forgiveness with you,
so that you may be revered. R.

I wait for the Lord, my soul waits,
and in his word I hope;
my soul waits for the Lord
more than those who watch for the morning. R.

# ⌒ Saturday, the First Week

Deuteronomy 26:16–19; Matthew 5:43–48

*Love your enemies and pray for those who persecute you,*
*so that you may be children of your Father in heaven;*
*for he makes his sun rise on the evil and on the good.*

The cover story of a recent issue of *Newsweek* magazine was entitled "The Biology of Beauty: What Science Has Discovered About Sex Appeal." Like much research, it confirmed what our instincts already know and what most folks' fantasies create. Large eyes, a small nose, and smooth and unblemished skin are among the hallmarks of female beauty according to the study. Height, a strong chin, and musculature are among the desirable male qualities. Not so terribly startling.

What seemed to be intriguing, however, as well as unsuspected, was the factor of symmetry. The more the right half of someone's face and body is mirrored by the left half, the more beautiful that person tends to be considered. If love at first sight ever happens, all of this is part of the brushwork.

In contrast, the gospel's hallmark for love is care for one's enemies, prayerful concern for the persecutor, the hassler, for the one we would like to airbrush out of life's portrait. In a society as pervasive and expansive as ours, yet also as intrusive and inescapable as it is (due to our media-hungry culture), too often the anonymous other becomes that enemy. We find ourselves warring against those on welfare, the jobless minority, the dependent immigrant, the uneducated, the street person. They become our enemies, though we would be hardpressed to name one or identify one in a line-up of similarly dressed individuals or perhaps even able to admit we have ever spoken with one. Yet they become our enemies—the unknown, the anonymous, those relegated to class dismissal. They are the ones whom we perceive to ruin the beauty of our society. They upset the balance and distort the symmetry.

In a culture of beauty-by-measurement, the anonymous ones then become the enemy whom believers embrace with gospel love: the street person we take the time to get to know, the unwanted child adopted, the vote for a political candidate who cares for the weak, the immigrant given a job, the minority person welcomed as a neighbor, the welfare program supported, the house built with Habitat for

26

Humanity. Each person and each deed becomes a Charlie Brown Christmas tree, beautiful in the imperfection others are inclined to bestow, a once-upon-a-time enemy beloved. Such are the times we find ourselves with new eyes and a new sense of balance and harmony, God's asymmetrical perfection.

*Name for yourself a time when you were able to see with your heart, beyond the symmetry. How do you make sure you are not captivated solely by the beauty of perfection? How do you cultivate love for the anonymous other?*

## Prayer • psalm 119

R. Happy are they who follow the law of the Lord!

Happy are those whose way is blameless,
who walk in the law of the Lord.
Happy are those who keep his decrees,
who seek him with their whole heart. R.

You have commanded your precepts
to be kept diligently.
O that my ways may be steadfast
in keeping your statutes! R.

I will praise you with an upright heart,
when I learn your righteous ordinances.
I will observe your statutes;
do not utterly forsake me. R.

# The Second Week of Lent

# ·⟋· The Second Sunday

Year A: Genesis 12:1–4; 2 Timothy 1:8–10; Matthew 17:1–9
Year B: Genesis 22:1–2, 9–13, 15–18; Romans 8:31–34; Mark 9:2–10
Year C: Genesis 15:5–12, 17–18; Philippians 3:17—4:1; Luke 9:28–36

*Jesus took with him Peter and John and James,*
*and went up on the mountain to pray.*

Prayer tends to be a very personal thing for most of us. Some would say that it is talking to God, though I should rather think that prayer is being a part of what happens on the mountaintop where even the sun grows dazzled and all that is tattered turns light and regal. It is a transfiguration of sorts within a moment's cloud of Godly wonder and awe, and it happens to most of us at least once or twice or thrice in our lives. Then it echoes and spirals forth forever like hoops of God settling about our shoulders. And every once in a while we glimpse our way back. I think that is what prayer is — glimpsing our way back.

Love is found on mountaintops, or stumbled upon, or fallen into, or flown like a kite catching the passion that swirls about the crest. And in the end it is lived there with all its jagged peaks and crevices but also with all the sunrises and sunsets your passion can bear. Yes, the mountaintop is passionate love, and it is prayer.

And it is all the colors of autumn on the mountaintop, browns dappled in orange pumpkins and drizzled with new red apples and burnished gold. It is springtime on the mountaintop, as well, borne on the scent of new life, and trees yawning with buds as they nudge themselves out of hibernation. And it is summer, too, delightfully lazy and listless. And winter, crunching and crackling with crisp light. Yes, the mountaintop is the best of every season unraveling into your lap, and it is prayer.

It is poetry, too, that is written on mountaintops. Not just rhyming verses, but words that sing all by themselves, words with a universe in their soul and rhythm that brings a dancing beat to the strutting of your heart. Yes, the mountaintop is poetry, and it is prayer.

It is death that finally comes home to roost on the mountaintop and admits it has all been a joke as laughter rolls out of its mouth and down the mountainsides until all the villages in the valleys beneath are spilling over in laughter because now everyone knows the joke—that death never had any power at all. And resurrection simply stands alone at the top and smiles. Yes the mountaintop is forever, and it is prayer.

Only you and I and the Lord cannot live there forever—at least not yet, and so we make our way down the mountainside and back among the rubble of our lives, down from the poetry and the passion, down into the everyday living where springtime forgets to come and winter is gray slush and autumn is stripped bare. That is where we do most of our living, at the bottom of the mountain; but that rubble is also the foothills of the place where once we met our God and where our minds spun in unimaginable wonder and where we wished we could build booths to stay forever.

Sometimes the struggle among the rubble is too great and we grow discouraged. And sometimes it is too demanding and we grow distracted. And sometimes it goes on too long and we forget. But then someone always wonders aloud what it means to rise from the dead. And then someone else remembers the mountaintop and tells the story — and that is all that matters, to remember we were once there and will be once again. And it is prayer.

*Name a mountaintop in your life. How was God there with you? How did it change your life, if indeed it did? Did you find different priorities? greater peace? stronger faith? a still point?*

### Prayer • psalm 27

R. The Lord is my light and my salvation.

Hear, O Lord, when I cry aloud,
be gracious to me and answer me!
"Come," my heart says, "seek his face!"
Your face, Lord, do I seek. R.

Do not hide your face from me.
Do not turn your servant away in anger,
you who have been my help.
Do not cast me off, do not forsake me. R.

I believe that I shall see the goodness of the Lord
in the land of the living.
Wait for the Lord; be strong,
and let your heart take courage. R.

# ✐ Monday, the Second Week

Daniel 9:4–10; Luke 6:36–38

> *Jesus said to his disciples: "Be merciful,*
> *just as your Father is merciful."*

For a good portion of this century Cadillac defined quality in automotive engineering, so much so that the word "cadillac" came to describe excellence in quality for just about anything. In much the same way, Babe Ruth defined for countless generations what it meant to be a baseball player. It was Jesus, however, who defined once and for all what it means to be human.

St. Paul recognized Jesus as the first human being simply because he saw Jesus as the one who so totally lived out his humanity. For Paul, Jesus is Lord, the one who lived among us as unconditional love and unlimited mercy and the fullness of life. He was compassion itself, and justice and gentleness and goodness and wholeness. And by being such Jesus established for us all what it means to be truly human, and thus he became Lord of all life. Only you and I and everyone else have not yet matched that standard, which is not to say that we have failed but only that it is a lifelong journey of struggling to grow into his image. Maya Angelou says it yet another way:

> Many things continue to amaze me, even well into the sixth decade of my life. I'm startled or taken aback when people walk up to me and tell me they are Christians. My first response is the question "Already?" It seems to me a lifelong endeavor to try to live the life of a Christian. I believe that is also true for the Buddhist, for the Muslim, for the Jainist, for the Jew, and for the Taoist who try to live their beliefs. The idyllic condition cannot be arrived at and held on to eternally (*Wouldn't Take Nothing for My Journey Now*).

And so in the end we come to realize that it takes a lot of living to even come close to being human the way Jesus was.

Now, I have no difficulty with those who say they cannot be compassionate in his image, or always forgiving, or willing to pardon, or generous and giving. I suppose I have no difficulty with them simply because I myself am not able to be all that he was. On occasion, perhaps. All of us capture a sliver of his light at times. But all of the time?

even most of the time? No.

I do confess some difficulty, however, with those who profess to be disciples of his, yet seem to conclude that the Lord Jesus does not call us to live life in such a totally human fashion. It is with those folks that I struggle, for it seems to me that to be a disciple is to accept the call to be human, fully human, in all that that means. In saying yes to that call, you and I begin the endless journey.

*Since Jesus defined what it means for us to be human, then any-thing which causes us to be less than human, any choice or any action or any value that is dehumanizing, would be sinful. How does that understanding affect your concept of sin? How does it affect your understanding of grace?*

## Prayer • psalm 79

R. Lord, do not deal with us as our sins deserve.

Do not remember against us
the iniquities of our ancestors;
let your compassion come speedily to meet us,
for we are brought very low. R.

Help us, O God of our salvation,
for the glory of your name;
deliver us, and forgive our sins,
for your name's sake. R.

Let the groans of the prisoners come before you;
according to your great power preserve those doomed to die.
Then we your people, the flock of your pasture,
will give thanks to you forever;
from generation to generation
we will recount your praise. R.

# ☝ Tuesday, the Second Week

Isaiah 1:10, 16–20; Matthew 23:1–12

*Cease to do evil, learn to do good; seek justice,*
*rescue the oppressed, defend the widow.*

Thomas Jefferson was a dreamer and a visionary, like Joan of Arc in France and like Walt Whitman would come to be. While an idealist of amazing proportions, however, Jefferson also lived a life of contradictions which were just as extraordinary.

Along with other notables, Thomas Jefferson drafted the American experiment and penned it into the Declaration of Independence, proclaiming that "all men are created equal," and that all therefore should be guaranteed "life, liberty, and the pursuit of happiness." Yet Jefferson himself owned hundreds of slaves who served him at Monticello. On the one hand he brought to this land an industrial vision which attempted to free its citizens from oppressive labor practices, yet because of his personal needs for financial funds he operated a small nail factory by the labor of slave youths. In much the same way Jefferson sought a new nation free of the powers of big government, yet the Louisiana Purchase was brought about by his presidency without ever being completely authorized by the legislative Congress. Thomas Jefferson was indeed a dreamer, but he was also someone who lived out that dream immersed in many contradictions.

On the other hand, don't we all. Two people enter a marriage and promise to one another and before the faith community, "I will love you forever—no matter what." Yet finding the light through that "no matter what" is scattered with all sorts of shadows and dim wanderings and hide-and-go-seek game playing. We hedge our bets.

The church is not necessarily much better at living out the vision. We call for a just world and profess to stand for the weakest in the human community, yet at times the church's own justice is frail and faint toward those within the church itself—toward church employees and women and theologians who seek a fair hearing.

So we live with one another and with ourselves—all flawed, yet dreamers nonetheless. And in our many contradictions, it is not that our dreams are crippled; only that you and I lack the wholeness to enflesh them as we might hope. But that does not make the dreams any less or us any more the hypocrites—not Thomas Jefferson, not those who marry, not the church which seeks to be holy. No, the dreams are our light. They stand out ahead of us as a beacon, for that is where dreams are meant to be. Then you and I and everyone else stumble along as best we can, for without the dreams we would be lost in the dark.

Dreams are how our God teaches us, or are at least one of the ways our God teaches us. Certainly the Word of God is a lamp unto our feet. And the wisdom of the faith community gathered over the centuries, that is a way of being taught as well. But dreams, too, are God teaching us what we might be, whether they be the dreams of Thomas Jefferson or Walt Whitman or Joan of Arc, whether they be of those within the church or those outside the church, whether they be of saints or of flawed sinners. We are all scribes and Pharisees in so many ways, and we are all learners sitting as the feet of the master and teacher who is both Lord and Messiah.

*What are the contradictions in your life? What are the dreams tempered by compromise? How are your visions of what could be muddied by what is? How do you keep your dreams alive?*

## Prayer • psalm 50

R. To the upright I will show the saving power of God.

Not for your sacrifices do I rebuke you;
your burnt offerings are continually before me.
I will not accept a bull from your house,
or goats from your folds. R.

What right have you to recite my statutes,
or take my covenant on your lips?
For you hate discipline,
and you cast my words behind you. R.

Those who bring thanksgiving
as their sacrifice honor me;
to those who go the right way
I will show the salvation of God. R.

# ⚡ Wednesday, the Second Week

Jeremiah 18:18–20; Matthew 20:17–28

*Whoever wishes to be great among you must be your servant, and whoever wishes to be first among you must be your slave.*

Despite what some might claim, the purpose of going to school is not to one day graduate. The purpose, it would seem, is to learn. The fact that those who are successful at learning also graduate does not change the equation. School is about learning and not about graduating. The latter is simply the formal conclusion to the prior.

The same might be said of marriage. Two people do not marry so that they can live together—or at least that should not be their overriding purpose, though that may be a motive somewhere in the mix of things. Rather, what marriage should be about is the mutual support and nurturing care the two individuals bring to one another. Like the learning which culminates in graduation, a couple may, in the process, grow to be so united that living together becomes only an externalization of what is taking place deep within. In other words, a united love happens because of the care and support and struggle.

The order of such priorities has taken me a long time to learn—longer than I would care to admit. What brought it all home was learning that the purpose of life is not to make me happy, that life is not here to serve me, but rather for me to serve life, and if I do that, then I will be happy. Or to put it in the context of faith, the purpose of life is for me to serve the God who is Life, and not the other way around. As I said, it is taken me a long time to learn that, and the fact is that I need to keep learning it simply because I keep forgetting it. Then, when I start thrashing about because life isn't going my way, sooner or later (though it is mostly later, if I'm honest) I remember what I learned once before. So then, I learn it again for the umpteenth time. Life is not here to serve me, but I am here to serve life, i.e., God.

I take some comfort (not much, but a little) in the fact that this is not a new struggle for human beings. Long ago it was the struggle for Zebedee's two boys, and for Zebedee's wife too who came to Jesus as an advocate for her sons, hoping that the fruit of her womb might sit on the right and left hands of God. And Jesus' response was simply,

"I can't give them that. I can only give them the journey—the learning part, the nurturing and caring part. The graduation (of sorts) belongs to my Father."

So it seems, then, that at least according to Jesus life is not about saving our souls—the *Baltimore Catechism* notwithstanding. Life is about serving, and in the process we will save our souls, if that is what we are wondering about. But again, salvation is for the Father to give.

The difference is that we end up living life differently. If we are about saving our souls, we tend to think that saying prayers and going to Mass and belonging to the right religion is important, and that is where we then put our energies. If we are about serving, however, then we spend our time with other folks, with those who need to be served. It is true—in the process we get worn out, but that is just when our God comes and offers us a place to sit down and rest, either on the right or on the left.

*Write out a mission statement for your life. Or to put it another way, write out the purpose of living as you understand it. Do you tend to view life as here for you, or that you are here for life's needs?*

## Prayer • psalm 31

R. Save me, O Lord, in your steadfast love.

Take me out of the net that is hidden for me,
for you are my refuge.
Into your hand I commit my spirit;
you have redeemed me, O Lord, faithful God. R.

For I hear the whispering of many—
terror all around!—
as they scheme together against me.
as they plot to take my life. R.

But I trust in you, O Lord;
I say, "You are my God."
My times are in your hand;
deliver me from the hand
of my enemies and persecutors. R.

# ∿ Thursday, the Second Week

Jeremiah 17:5–10; Luke 16:19–31

*Between you and us a great chasm has been fixed, so that*
*those who might want to pass from here to you cannot do so,*
*and no one can cross from there to us.*

Life has a way of carving chasms across our lives. Or maybe it is not life that does the trenching but we who do so, except that too many of us never notice until the abyss is so wide and so deep that we cannot go back. The host of a radio talk show the other day commented that he had never heard anyone on their deathbed lament that they had not spent more time at the office. The unspoken part of the lament seemed to be that many do regret not having spent more time with those they love, and that on one's deathbed there is no longer any going back. Then the chasm has become too wide.

I suppose the issue should not be so much one of wondering if there are parts of life passing us by—life is too big, too grand, too generous to take it all in, to be attentive to it all. Rather, perhaps, the issue is one of learning to be attentive to the significant moments, all the while allowing the other portions to quietly find their own niche.

It is not unlike the issue of the rich man who dresses in purple and linen and feasts daily in much magnificence while Lazarus, sore-infested and draped in poverty, sits unnoticed in the shadow of the rich man's comings and goings. Somehow with a kind of busy blindness the rich man seems to have missed it all, missed it daily until when he finally does see, well then, the chasm of death has become irreversible.

In one way or another it happens to us all somewhere among our meanderings through life. We find ourselves caught in the snare of some addiction, caught without ever realizing its growing power. Or we discover ourselves blindsided by a divorce we never saw coming. Or we come to the backside of our lives and find it overflowing with the accumulations of a lifetime yet empty of any loves, and we wonder how that ever came to be. It makes little difference that *A Christmas Carol* is a tale told only once a year, but its Scrooge factor plays itself out all year long—that is, the difficulty of being brought to see before the chasm is too deep. How does one come to see when one is already blind, and others saying so only deepens the darkness?

There is a wisdom in the poet Jeremiah as he cautions against trusting solely in ourselves for then we shrivel and grow barren like a tree planted in lava waste. The one who is wise, admonishes the poet, trusts in the Lord. Such a person is like a tree planted at the shore of a fresh flowing stream. Such a one bears much fruit.

If Jeremiah be true, then the abundance which fosters self-sufficiency in us may indeed be a curse, for then each of us makes our own merry and inattentive way, blind to those who sit at our comings and goings. On the other hand, the neediness which nurtures dependence may be a blessing as then we are obligated to journey through life together, attentive to each other. In other words, in the midst of self-sufficient abundance, there is much out of which to dig a chasm. When there is little, there is also little to hide behind, and also much easier to see clearly.

*Name an abundance of yours which once seemed to be a blessing and which has now become a curse. Name a need which pushed you into dependence and which has now become a blessing.*

## Prayer • psalm 1

R. Happy are they who hope in the Lord.

Happy are those who do not follow
the advice of the wicked,
or take the path that sinners tread,
or sit in the seat of scoffers;
but their delight is in the law of the Lord,
and on his law they meditate day and night. R.

They are like trees planted by streams of water;
which yield their fruit in its season,
and their leaves do not wither.
In all that they do, they prosper. R.

The wicked are not so,
but are like chaff that the wind drives away.
For the Lord watches over the way of the righteous,
but the way of the wicked will perish. R.

# ·⸙ Friday, the Second Week

### Genesis 37:3–4, 12–13, 17–28; Matthew 21:33–43, 45–46

*He will put those wretches to a miserable death, and lease the vineyard*
*to other tenants who will give him the produce at the harvest time.*

In the master plan of God's unfolding love, salvation hung on a whim.

If Joseph's brothers had not sat around in a drowsy post-lunch lament of their familial status, Joseph would never have been tossed into a parched cistern. Had Joseph not been deep in a well there in the desert, he would not have been sold for twenty pieces of silver to a nomad caravan. Had that nomad caravan not been making its way to Egypt, Joseph would not ever have become the pharaoh's fair-haired dream counselor. Had Joseph not risen to status in the pharaoh's court, he would not have been able to provide a doorway out of hunger to his father and eleven brothers. Had Jacob and his clan not made their way to Egypt for a respite from hunger, the descendants of Abraham would never have settled there and eventually been edged into Egyptian slavery. Had there been no such servitude, neither would Moses have ever cried, "Let my people go!" Had Moses not dreamed the dream, there would have been no exodus, and without an exodus there would have been no desert. Without the desert, Sinai would not have become a beacon to Moses' band of lost souls, and had they not gathered at Sinai there would have been no ten commandments. Without the decalogue, there would have been no covenant. Without the covenant, no promised land. Without the nation, no people of David. And without the people of promise, there would have been no fulfillment in Jesus. So it is that in the master plan of God's unfolding love, salvation hung on the spontaneous whim of a handful of jealous brothers.

Yet as often as our lives seem out of control (whether it seems to be out of our control or God's), the fact is that the big screen version of human history in the end tells the tale of a God who refuses to abandon the vineyard to ragtag and indifferent hoodlums. Chance seems not to be in the repertoire of God's love. Whether by design or by precarious whim, God weaves it all into a future she has dreamed.

In these days, some folk (usually those who seem to have lost their dreams) lament what to them seems to be a younger generation wallowing in lost faith. Yet they may not have lost their faith. It may well be that these young people have simply not lived long enough to recognize the jigsaw puzzle being fit together. In time they will, as have generations before them, as will generations who follow them. God's vineyard has not been abandoned. The grapes have been pressed. The wine has been poured, and the glass has been raised. God awaits the toast.

*Daydream about your life to date. Take some time to recognize the pieces coming together. What pieces still need more time to fit in? How is the picture different than you would have ever imagined? How is it the same?*

## Prayer • psalm 105

R. Remember the marvels the Lord has done.

When God summoned famine against the land,
and broke every staff of bread,
he had sent a man ahead of them,
Joseph, who was sold as a slave. R.

His feet were hurt with fetters,
his neck was put in a collar of iron;
until what he had said came to pass,
the word of the Lord kept testing him. R.

The king sent and released him;
the ruler of the peoples set him free.
He made him lord of his house,
and ruler of all his possessions. R.

# ✓ Saturday, the Second Week

Micah 7:14–15, 18–20; Luke 15:1–3, 11–32

*Jesus told them this parable: "There was a man who had two sons."*

We are at heart, all of us, seekers and searchers. For some of us what we ultimately pursue is stability, permanence, security—a rock hard place on which to stand and from which we can view life as it passes by. For others it is excitement, living at the edge, life ever new—eagle's wings to soar. Some folks even hunger for both, curiously—love at home and passion on the road.

Most of us, it seems, want more of what we already have—more roots to withstand the forces which bend and loosen, or more wind currents to soar lest the snares tie us to the earth. So at some point in life we pack up the inheritance bestowed by our genes, psyches, and spirits and set off seeking either more security or more excitement, not knowing where the quest will take us but also believing we'll know when we arrive. Now, the Jungian shadow side of who we are would advise us not to pursue more of what we already are but rather more of the lesser and so come to some sort of balance. But that seems to us to be unnatural, and so we go with what seem to be our conscious hungers.

Like the youngest son of the prodigal father, we spend the inheritance of our lives seeking what our hearts desire. In the end all such quests leave us impoverished in one way or the other. Yet it is that emptiness which then also becomes our grace. Having tried it all and with nowhere else to go we finally make our way back to where we began the journey, or back to the one with whom we began. After a lifetime of seeking, we eventually confess our emptiness, mostly to ourselves but also to the power of Life within our silent selves. It is then that we come home.

It is the story, as well, of how our God shepherds us and does so in curious fashion by not shepherding us. It is the tale of a God who brings us to where we need to be through the rhythms of life simply because our God is the very rhythm of life waiting to be recognized as such.

Some, like the younger son, come to that place early on; and some, like the elder son, struggle toward that recognition, fighting it all along the way. And while it seems some people never come to that point, it may just be for them that the gift of death is the final point

42

of conversion which, at one and the same time, empties us of all our pursuits and fills us with that which we have always sought. So then death becomes the greatest of all graces, the means by which we are both ultimately rooted without any fear as well as able to live at the edge of an evolving future, simply because that future is our God.

*Name the portions of life which you have tried and found wanting. Then name those portions which you still want. Where in the story of the father's two sons would you place yourself?*

## Prayer • psalm 103

R. The Lord is kind and merciful.

Bless the Lord, O my soul,
and all that is within me, bless his holy name.
Bless the Lord, O my soul,
and do not forget all his benefits. R.

The Lord, who forgives all your iniquity,
who heals all your diseases,
who redeems your life from the Pit,
who crowns you with steadfast love and mercy. R.

The Lord will not always accuse,
nor will he keep his anger forever.
He does not deal with us according to our sins,
nor repay us according to our iniquities. R.

For as the heavens are high above the earth,
so great is his steadfast love toward those who fear him;
as far as the east is from the west,
so far the Lord removes our transgressions from us. R.

# The Third
# Week
# of Lent

# ✐ The Third Sunday (Year A)

Exodus 17:3–7; Romans 5:1–2, 5–8; John 4:5–42

*Jesus said, "Everyone who drinks of this water will be thirsty again,*
*but those who drink of the water that I will give them*
*will never be thirsty. The water I will give will become in them a*
*spring of water gushing up to eternal life."*

The magazine section of the local Sunday paper recently devoted a column to asking teenagers what one question they would like to know the answer to. Like fireworks, a spray of questions exploded out of the darkness of their lives. You might expect some of the questions: "What is the one thing every woman looks for in a man?" Others flowed from life's pain, as they do for each of us: "Why did my grandma die of cancer?" and "Why does love hurt so much?"

The one that stayed with me the longest was "Will I ever be rich enough to be happy in my life?" Oh, probably not, I thought to myself. Yet I think the question stayed with me for such a time simply because there is so much sadness in it. When you are young it seems there is never enough of anything to make you happy, and so happiness will seem to be far away. And when you are old, well, if you have great muchness, you are likely to have missed having someone to share it with in the chase to have enough. Thus the pursuit of enough always seems so elusive, perhaps because happiness is less a commodity and more a by-product of lived love.

If the young man who asked that question is fortunate, someone will enter his life who will distract him from the quest and introduce him to greater and more worthwhile realms. And if he is blessed further he will allow himself to explore that unknown, like the story of the woman whose path crossed with Jesus' at Jacob's well in Samaria. She came looking for one thing, in this instance water for the day, something with which to cook and do her dishes and satisfy her thirst. What she ended up finding was that which satisfies a much deeper thirst, that is, for meaning and understanding and ultimately some Godliness in her life. She found what she never really came seeking for, only to realize it was what she had wanted all along.

We so easily become distracted by the more obvious quests, like the desert people of this week's first reading who go grumbling to Moses because there is no water. Oh, they needed water to survive, just as we all come issued with basic needs that scream for attention. The challenge, however, is always to recognize the quieter but greater needs, those that belong to our spirits and not just to our bodies. Too often we seek the obvious only because there is a much deeper spirit for which out souls yearn.

For the woman, it is that recognition of a much deeper thirst that unfolds into a clearer vision of her own life. "You are right in saying, 'I have no husband'; for you have had five husbands." It is then that the conversation moves on to the realization that God is not about dwelling here or there but that "God is spirit and those who worship him must worship in spirit and truth" (John 4:24), which is another way of talking about love or solitude or beauty, all a touch of Godliness in our lives.

So will the young man who wonders if he will ever be rich enough ever be happy? Probably not, if what he really wants is happiness, simply because he'll be looking in all the wrong places. Yet somewhere along the way, I suspect someone will come along and in some offhand way invite him to consider another possibility toward happiness. And if he is willing to explore the possibility, like the woman at the Samaritan well, then maybe he will find his way into what he is truly thirsting for. Maybe then he will.

*When have you gone looking for something in life only to come upon a deeper and richer grace? What current thirst of yours brings you to life's well?*

## ⟡ Prayer • psalm 95

R. If today you hear his voice, harden not your hearts.

O come, let us sing to the Lord;
let us make a joyful noise to the rock of our salvation!
Let us come into his presence with thanksgiving;
let us make a joyful noise to him with songs of praise! R.

O come, let us worship and bow down,
let us kneel before the Lord, our Maker!
For he is our God,
and we are the people of his pasture,
and the sheep of his hand. R.

# ✐ The Third Sunday (Year B)

Exodus 20:1–17; 1 Corinthians 1:22–25; John 2:13–25

*For Jews demand signs and Greeks desire wisdom, but we proclaim*
*Christ crucified, a stumbling block to Jews and foolishness to Gentiles.*

One of the saddest of all things is to come to the end of one's life and discover one had never taken a stand on anything. I don't mean not having an opinion about something. Anybody can have an opinion, and just about everyone does. I mean not taking a stand.

Stands are different. They cost us something, and usually bring a fair amount of pain somewhere along the way. They can be divisive, too, and get people hollering at each other, and slip in under your skin like a sliver that begins to fester round about everything else that needs doing. But stands can also unite. They can galvanize around a cause or around a dream or sometimes even around a love. Stands can do good things. Opinions just itch, mostly like mosquito bites.

When Joshua asks the elders in the first reading this weekend where they stand on God, and when Jesus asks the disciples in the gospel where they stand on him, I can feel myself getting a bit nervous. What if someone decides to ask me where I stand? But mostly no one ever asks, mainly because asking always entertains the risk of the other person turning the question on the one who began it all. So few people ever ask. Just about all of us would rather slip out from under having to take a stand.

There is something freeing about taking a stand, however, though at first glance that may seem to be a contradiction. Once you and I know where we stand, we no longer have to cover all the bases, no longer have to hedge our bets, no longer have to play the entire field. A commitment gives direction and focus and frees us from fooling around on the periphery. In a kaleidoscope world where all the pieces keep tumbling, a stand declares the center, and that does free us from wondering where else to stand.

So every once in a while you and I and a lot of other people of faith choose to stand up and be counted. (And once in a while is maybe as often as we can do it simply because it does cost.) When minorities move into our neighborhood we stand up to fears of declining property values and choose not to move out. When others bulldoze the poor we stand firm in support of the weakest. When just and moral

48

business practices debate corporate profitability over the issues of where to invest we stand on our consciences. When we tinker with compromise for the sake of a promotion we decide to stand for the values of Jesus instead. Such are times when stands cost. Most folks have opinions; believers take stands.

Indeed, there are others too who take stands—upon comfort or profit or even upon a salt shaker's worth of glitter. But stands taken by believers are taken with a different vision, one of spirit, simply because we have come to recognize that it is the spirit that gives life and not the flesh, as Jesus was wont to remind us.

*How do others consider you, as someone with opinions or someone who is willing to take a stand? Remember a time when you took a stand. What did it cost you? Was it freeing? Would you do it again?*

## Prayer • psalm 19

R. Lord, you have the words of everlasting life.

The law of the Lord is perfect,
reviving the soul;
the decrees of the Lord are sure,
making wise the simple. R.

The precepts of the Lord are right,
rejoicing the heart;
the commandment of the Lord is clear,
enlightening the eyes. R.

The fear of the Lord is pure,
enduring forever;
the ordinances of the Lord are true
and righteous altogether. R.

More to be desired are they than gold,
even much fine gold;
sweeter also than honey,
and drippings of the honeycomb. R.

49

# ✒ The Third Sunday (Year C)

Exodus 3:1–8, 13–15; 1 Corinthians 10:1–6, 10–12; Luke 13:1–9

*The gardener replied, "Sir, let it alone for one more year, until I dig*
*around it and put manure on it. If it bears fruit next year,*
*well and good; but if not, you can cut it down."*

Manager Tom Trebelhorn of the Milwaukee Brewers baseball team was fond of saying that every baseball problem resolved itself in ten days. (Well, actually I only heard him say it once.) Given the fact that he is no longer manager of the Milwaukee Brewers, however, his wisdom may be somewhat suspect. Obviously some things did not get resolved according to his timetable. Yet it is also true that none of our calendars seem to be able to map the unfolding future.

Outcomes do tend to function according to their own schedule, indifferent to the energy we put forth. There certainly are times when more effort does not seem to spur the process toward fruitfulness. Or if it does, the desired results are so far distant that it becomes nigh impossible to do any measuring. It seems to happen throughout all of life.

Parents painfully scan the horizon of their children's lives in search of some faint silhouette of faith, yet frequently wonder if their efforts have made any difference. Married couples muddle about in their relationships, endlessly offering love upon love in hopes that something will begin to be woven into a recognizable marriage, even if it is scattered with snags and frayed ends. If in the end it is difficult to recognize as a marriage, it certainly isn't for lack of trying.

Parishioners find parish life gouged and carved by bitter and angry winds of parish infighting while they endlessly search for a way into some sort of ecclesial springtime. Amazingly, they continue to work on councils and committees, share faith, and make eucharist. Communities refuse to surrender their neighborhoods as well as their dreams to violence or racism or fear or injustice. Incapable of escaping the failure, they feel compelled to embrace it and so struggle even more to build upon it.

The gospel parable is the tale of a vineyard owner who spends three years of patience upon a fig tree that bears only barren promises, and then he allows himself to be persuaded into waiting even longer. The craziness of the story is that it has no ending. We never do find out what happens.

Traditional biblical commentary would have us recognize there the patience of God in face of human sinfulness. It is, however, also a story of human patience in the face of a divine calendar that promises forthcoming but distant fruit.

If God waits upon us, it is also we who wait upon God. If God fertilizes the handiwork of our lives, it is also our efforts that fertilize the stirrings of divine life struggling to be what it is meant to be. If God wonders why there is no fruit in our lives, it is also we who wonder where God's fruit is in our lives. If the parable is God's story about us, it is also our story about God.

The Scriptures are filled with stories of emptiness overflowing with divine abundance, yet all in its own good time. Deserts bloom but only after exile, barren wombs bear new life though it be in old age, blind folks do come to see, mere youths slay long-threatening giants, and the dead do find life though only after dying. In each case an endlessly barren bush bears so much fruit that it burns feverishly without ever being consumed. If Jesus comes to say anything, it is that all of life is rooted in ground so holy that fruit does come forth.

*Have there been aspects of your life in which fruit has not come forth despite your best efforts? What sort of faith conclusions have you drawn? What others might you have drawn?*

## Prayer • psalm 103

R. The Lord is kind and merciful.

God forgives all your iniquity,
heals all your diseases,
redeems your life from the pit,
and crowns you with steadfast love and mercy. R.

The Lord works vindication and justice
for all who are oppressed.
He made known his ways to Moses,
his acts to the people of Israel. R.

The Lord is merciful and gracious,
slow to anger and abounding in steadfast love.
For as the heavens are high above the earth,
so great is his steadfast love
toward those who fear him. R.

# Monday, the Third Week

2 Kings 5:1–15; Luke 4:24–30

*Jesus said, "Truly I tell you, no prophet is accepted in the prophet's hometown." They got up and drove him out of the town.*

In the process of raising children, a thick slice of the loaf is bringing children to see what they would clearly rather not see. They resist it, fight it, ignore it, and deny it. And yet without it they (and we before them) never begin the journey of becoming human. That "it" is about healthy eating habits and getting enough sleep and good manners and being honest and sharing and saying "thank you" and not lying or stealing and recognizing the value of work and its necessity. There is something about being a kid that does not want to know all such things, that perceives it all as taking the fun out of life. We were the same way, and kids are that way today; and as much as we needed someone to show us, so they, too, need someone to teach them.

Current thinking suggests that we have about eighteen years to bring each generation to the point of human readiness, and that once they have reached the age of eighteen the task is completed. Consequently, we do not hesitate to correct or admonish a ten-year-old, yet someone who is twenty years of age—well, we are a bit hesitant, as if they should know better and who are we to tell someone what is right or wrong, good or bad.

Yet the truth is that the process of becoming fully human takes a full lifetime—and then some. All that is life-giving and death-dealing never seems to be fully obvious. That is why we keep on making mistakes, sometimes the same ones over and over again. It is also why we need prophets, why Naaman needed Elisha and why the citizens of Nazareth needed Jesus. We all need people in our lives who see what we do not and who are willing to say it even when we do not want to hear it, even when we are angry because of it. We need prophets who are honest with us. It is why we keep coming back to faith, coming back to the Lord Jesus.

*Do you allow Scripture to confront you? What was the most recent issue over which the Word of God brought you to change your way of thinking? What are the portions of your value system that are biblically based?*

## Prayer • psalm 42

R. My soul is thirsting for the living God;
when shall I see him face to face?

As a deer longs for flowing streams,
so my soul longs for you, O God.
My soul thirsts for God, for the living God.
When shall I come and behold the face of God? R.

O send out your light and your truth;
let them lead me;
let them bring me to your holy mountain
and to your dwelling. R.

Then I will go to the altar of God,
to God my exceeding joy;
and I will praise you with the harp,
O God, my God. R.

# ✧ Tuesday, the Third Week

Daniel 3:25, 34–43; Matthew 18:21–35

*Peter came and said to Jesus, "Lord, if a brother or sister sins against me, how often should I forgive? As many as seven times?"*

Robert Fulghum told us, "All I really need to know I learned in kindergarten," in a book by that same title. What he learned were such qualities as "play fair, wash your hands before you eat, clean up your own mess, flush, warm cookies and cold milk are good for you," and any number of other such life-wisdoms. Robert Fulghum begins his list with "share everything." This is something we all learned in the process of growing up, or should have, sharing toys and candy bars and the sandbox and whatever else it might have been that we had been given. It is a wisdom most of us live by.

Somewhere along the way, however, we also begin to realize that "share everything" is bigger than the sandbox and begs to include such things as time and love and skills we are good at. We even find ourselves sharing in other people's pain and suffering, in their laughter and in their tears. Share everything means just that—everything. It has also come to include forgiveness.

Sidney Callahan makes the point that forgiveness is the most difficult thing we ever have to do, and I suspect she is right about that. At least it is one of the most difficult things I find myself coming to terms with. It was Gandhi who recognized that forgiveness was not a characteristic of the weak but always of the strong. It is not easy to forgive. So when we come to realize that *share everything* includes sharing forgiveness, it isn't surprising that we can grow faint of heart.

I do not know that we ever feel like forgiving. Most of the time we find ourselves choosing to do so, or at times even faking it. We are still hurt and bruised; our feelings are still stinging. But we find we have to go on with life, and so we fake it. We pretend to forgive while nursing our wounds. Yet the pretending becomes a balm, a healing potion which soothes the cut.

And if we cannot do even that much, even fake it, even find ourselves at least *wishing* we could—which is already well on the way into forgiving—then maybe we have not really known forgiveness ourselves, or allowed ourselves to know it. That is the sadness of Jesus' parable about the servant who was forgiven a lifetime of debt but was unable to forgive a daytime of debt to another. To be really freed from our own sin, it seems, our own heart needs to be touched in such a way that it is able to free others from their sin. And if we are unable to do that, perhaps someone's lavish forgiveness of us has all been wasted.

Share everything, writes Robert Fulghum. Forgive as you have been forgiven, advises Jesus. And so we find ourselves wondering if our own hearts have yet been freed.

*Is extending forgiveness to another difficult for you? Remember a time when you found it really hard to forgive someone. Why was that so? What was the perceived price for you? Have you forgiven that person yet?*

## Prayer • psalm 25

R. Remember your mercies, O Lord.

Make me to know your ways, O Lord;
teach me your paths.
Lead me in your truth, and teach me,
for you are the God of my salvation. R.

Be mindful of your mercy, O Lord,
and of your steadfast love,
for they have been from of old.
Do not remember the sins of my youth
or my transgressions;
According to your steadfast love remember me,
for the sake of your goodness, O Lord! R.

Good and upright is the Lord;
therefore he instructs sinners in the way.
He leads the humble in what is right,
and teaches the humble his way. R.

# ✐ Wednesday, the Third Week

Deuteronomy 4:1, 5–9; Matthew 5:17–19

*Take care and watch yourselves closely, so as neither*
*to forget the things that your eyes have seen nor to*
*let them slip from your mind all the days of your life.*

While creationists and evolutionists have sparred with one another over how it all began and how it is that the human race got from that beginning moment to the now moment, Jesus' concern was about how it will all conclude and where it is that we are going and becoming. That *where* does not seem to have changed over the years. It is as if it has been written in Spirit even upon the most stony and hardened hearts.

Bridget spent three years in Japan teaching English as a second language. Then she decided to come back home and continue with her American life. In telling of her experiences Bridget spoke of how she found herself curiously surprised by Japanese parents saying the very same things to their children in Japanese that American parents say to their children in our tongue. "Share your toys." "Don't fight and push." "Be kind to one another." "Don't take what doesn't belong to you." Parents in the two cultures do not compare notes, yet the rules of raising good children seem fairly similar, instinctive even. The goodness for which parents hunger for their children seems to be pretty much the same wherever you go.

The book *Men Are from Mars, Women Are from Venus* by John Gray seeks to help us understand gender differences. In general, Gray tells us, men bond by shared activity; women bond by communicating. Men deal with stress by withdrawing (either into solitude or into activity) in order to reflectively sort through the dilemma. Women deal with stress by talking it through, thereby not only sorting out the issue but also their own feelings. Differences notwithstanding, the fact is that men and women both long to bond with other human beings. Both genders seek a life which is free of stress.

The point is that men and women go about seeking the same things in different ways. We may express our human desires differently, yet both women and men in one way or another seek to become peaceable, trusting, honest, kind, forgiving, joyful, filled with love.

Lent is about entering back into the process of becoming human, in case we have slipped out of it a bit. But more importantly, it is what Jesus was about 2000 years ago, and in fact is still about—moving through our souls and shaping our hearts into peace and trust and joy and love and all the other dreams he ever spun off into the human spirit. He came and still comes to fulfill what the Father always meant us to be, and not even the smallest part of these dreams will be stopped or set aside until they all come true. Why, our very hunger to be made new during this lenten season is proof in the pudding that he is still about this task—here and in Japan, in women and men both. The kingdom is in process of becoming and it will not be stopped, not one letter of the dream, not the smallest part of a letter.

*This Lent, what is it that you find yourself longing to become?*
*Where was the seed of this desire? How long has it been stirring?*

## Prayer • psalm 147

R. Praise the Lord, Jerusalem.

Praise the Lord, O Jerusalem!
Praise your God, O Zion!
For he strengthens the bars of your gates;
he blesses your children within you. R.

The Lord sends out his command to the earth;
his word runs swiftly.
He gives snow like wool;
he scatters frost like ashes. R.

The Lord declares his word to Jacob,
his statutes and ordinances to Israel.
He has not dealt thus with any other nation;
they do not know his ordinances. R.

# ✓ Thursday, the Third Week

Jeremiah 7:23–28; Luke 11:14–23

*Jesus said, "If it is by the finger of God that I cast out the demons, then the kingdom of God has come to you."*

Devils do not let go easily. They tend to be clingers and clutchers, and many are of the breed that only someone else can cast out. Yet most of us "someone elses" are hesitant to presume reaching into another person's life in order to cast out what we have decided is their devil. So most devils of whatever brand tend to hang on. For them, it all seems to work out fairly well.

Every Thursday afternoon there's a small handful of folks from the town in which I live who make a half-hour trek to the nearby state prison. Once there they spend two hours chit-chatting with a group of ten to fifteen prisoners soon to be released. It is a structured program intended to build bridges between prisoners and citizens so that the two can get to know one another a bit. Then, when the prisoners are released, there is someone in the community who becomes a trusted touchstone as the prisoners struggle to make good decisions about living on the outside.

It is a grassroots sort of reaching out. It is also a grassroots sort of reaching in on the part of the citizens, a reaching in to cast out some entrenched devils. Curiously, the prisoners are more willing than most people would be to let someone else try, in part because they themselves realize their own success rate has not been so great. So the prisoners are willing to allow someone to walk along with them.

What is amazing is the hope of this small band of local folks. They don't do what they do with any high expectations of success. They know full well that the prisoners' life-styles have deep roots, a lifetime of growing. The prisoners know that too. But what is so amazing is that both groups keep trying. And the citizens keep returning, even after a matchup has not been successful in keeping someone out of prison.

One man in the group said recently that he had never been paired with someone who did not return to prison. But he keeps going because he believes goodness is more powerful than evil, because he believes it's the group who succeeds and not the individual, because he believes that wherever there is even one success then there is the reign of God.

*Have you ever been a part of someone being freed from that which enslaved them? from something which possessed them? Appreciate those situations as the reign of God. Do you personally believe that goodness is more powerful than evil?*

### Prayer • psalm 95

R. If today you hear God's voice, harden not your hearts.

O come, let us sing to the Lord;
let us make a joyful noise to the rock of our salvation!
Let us come into his presence with thanksgiving;
let us make a joyful noise to him with songs of praise! R.

O come, let us worship and bow down,
let us kneel before the Lord, our maker!
For he is our God, and we are the people of his pasture,
and the sheep of his hand. R.

O that today you would listen to his voice!
do not harden your hearts, as at Meribah,
as on the day at Massah in the wilderness,
when your ancestors tested me, and put me to the proof,
though they had seen my work. R.

# ⌐ Friday, the Third Week

Hosea 14:2–10; Mark 12:28–34

*The scribe said to Jesus, "You are right, Teacher; 'to love him with
all the heart, and with all the understanding, and with all the
strength, and to love one's neighbor as oneself,' this is much more
important than all whole burnt offerings and sacrifices."*

Back in my college days when so much of life for me was still in the
process of becoming, I had a teacher who said, in the midst of one of
his lectures, that when he died he would prefer to be respected rather
than loved. It struck me as a strange wish back then, and maybe that
is why I still occasionally remember the comment now, thirty-five
years later—because what seemed strange then strikes me as strange
even now.

Why would someone wish to be respected rather than loved? And
if one follows the do-unto-others-as-you-wish-them-to-do-unto-you
principle, then I find myself wondering if that teacher worked at
respecting folks more than he did at loving them, which all seems to
be a bit of an inverted gospel, if you know what I mean.

It was Jesus who once challenged us to love God and our neighbor
as ourselves. He dropped it on us as a commandment then, and for a
lot of years I looked at it as just one more have-to. More recently,
though, I have begun to see it as something that God does in us,
something that happens to us if we are open to it. We find ourselves
wanting to become more loving, more caring—not just more lovable,
as we all do in the beginning of our love-life, but now more loving. It
is about a shift of direction, it seems to me, from "to me" to "out of
me," from receiving to giving. And I am not quite sure how or why
that shift happens—except that it does.

It may be another way of talking about what Erik Erikson wanted
us to understand regarding life tasks, how as children we need to first
develop a sense of trust, and then a sense of autonomy and initiative
and industry. Our adolescent task, he explained, is one of personal
identity, and as young adults it is one of achieving intimacy. Middle-
age is a call to generativity, and finally older adulthood to integration
and hope.

Maybe Erikson is putting flesh on the skeleton of Jesus' love command, that in the journey of our lives we find ourselves giving in to

our impulses to be more loving. Maybe it is less work and more surrender, a letting God do what God does best—which is bringing us to the love where we all begin in the first place. Perhaps that is why the gospel is called "good news" and why the church's prayer calls Lent a joyful season.

*Do you find yourself loving differently now than you once did? Why so? Has that change been your choice or was it something that occurred through other means?*

## Prayer • psalm 81

R. I am the Lord, your God: hear my voice.

I hear a voice I had not known:
"I relieved your shoulder of the burden;
your hands were freed from the basket.
In distress you called, and I rescued you. R.

"I answered you in the secret place of thunder;
I tested you at the waters of Meribah.
Hear, O my people, while I admonish you;
O Israel, if you would but listen to me! R.

"There shall be no strange god among you;
you shall not bow to a foreign god.
I am the Lord your God,
who brought you up out of the land of Egypt. R.

"O that my people would listen to me,
that Israel would walk in my ways!
I would feed you with the finest of the wheat,
and with honey from the rock I would satisfy you." R.

# ᐟᐣᐧ Saturday, the Third Week

Hosea 6:1–6; Luke 18:9–14

*Jesus told this parable: "Two men went up to the temple to pray,
one a Pharisee and the other a tax collector."*

How does one know what one needs? I am not talking of wants, but
needs. How does anyone know?

We were hiking the Grand Canyon along its northern rim and
making our way out to the tip of Bright Angel Point. The rim juts out
into the canyon maybe a quarter of a mile at that point. And like the
Christmas gift you hinted about for months and then became hopelessly resigned to not finding under the tree, only to discover it as the
last unwrapped gift, so the canyon on either side of this narrow point
is an amazing and breathless surprise. The only possible response is
one of awe and wonder akin to a divine silence.

As we were making our way back to the main portion of the rim
we passed others on the way out. One group was a family of five with
a daughter who was perhaps thirteen years old. "Da-a-ad," she plead-
ed, "can't we go? This isn't fun any more." What she *wanted* then was
to get on with the rest of their family vacation. She had seen enough
of the Grand Canyon. What she *needed*, however—well, that was
something else again. Perhaps what she needed was an appreciation
for the beauty of all that rushed up from below to embrace her.

When does one find that grace, for it is truly a gift? Her dad under-
stood, it seemed to me, that although an appreciation of beauty usually comes as we grow older, we still need to be exposed to it. In that
brief passing, he seemed to understand his daughter's want but also
her need to be exposed to beauty and one more experience of it.

We all know our wants: recognition from peers, comfortable living,
sexual excitement, *my* way of giving shape to life. What we are not
sure of, however, is how to uncover our needs. In some ways we are
not even sure we want to uncover them for fear of what they may call
us to hear. So then, given our own defenses against uncovering our
truest needs, how do we nevertheless do so? How does anyone know
their needs, be that me or you or the thirteen-year-old girl in need of
a sense of beauty?

Such unknowing was the sadness in the Pharisee of Luke's gospel.
He prayed in gratitude that he was not like so many others: grasping,

crooked, adulterous. It was a there-but-for-the-grace-of-God-go-I sort of prayer. The sadness there may well have been not knowing his needs, i.e., how and where he could be open to his God, what his life and his God were yet calling him to be. How does one enter into something when someone is not even conscious of the need to grow—like the thirteen-year-old girl and beauty? like the Pharisee?

On the other hand, the grace of Luke's tax collector was to know his need—a need for mercy. That too is also *our* hope—that if we (Pharisee or tax collector) strive to know the Lord, then the Lord will fill our needs, whatever they may be. As certain as the dawn in its coming, like the spring rains that water the earth, so the Lord will come to us. With Hosea, "let us strive to know the Lord"—there will we also come to recognize our needs.

*In your prayer, listen for a need calling out to you. Ask your God to enable you to hear.*

## ·⌒· Prayer • psalm 51

R. It is steadfast love, not sacrifice, that God desires.

Have mercy on me, O God,
according to your steadfast love;
according to your abundant mercy
blot out my transgressions.
Wash me thoroughly from my iniquity,
and cleanse me from my sin. R.

For you have no delight in sacrifice;
if I were to give a burnt offering,
you would not be pleased.
The sacrifice acceptable to God is a broken spirit;
a broken and contrite heart, O God,
you will not despise. R.

Do good to Zion in your good pleasure;
rebuild the walls of Jerusalem,
then you will delight in right sacrifices,
in burnt offerings and whole burnt offerings. R.

# The Fourth Week of Lent

# ◞ The Fourth Sunday (Year A)

1 Samuel 16:1, 6–7, 10–13; Ephesians 5:8–14; John 9:1–41

*Jesus said, "I came into this world for judgment so that those who do not see may see, and those who do see may become blind."*

On the Blackfeet Indian Reservation of northwestern Montana stands a mountain named Chief Mountain. It is bold and assertive and poised alone in the midst of the Rocky Mountain chain.

The guidebook points out that "for generations, native people have favored this impressive tower of ancient rock as a site for vision quests because it is thought to be the home of the Thunder Bird or perhaps the Wind Spirit. During such a quest, the vision seeker finds an isolated spot, calls upon the spirits for a dream of power and waits—often for days, and often without food or water. Among the Blackfeet, the spirit traditionally comes in the form of an animal or some natural force, such as thunder, which give some of their power to the seeker. It also teaches the seeker to tap this power with songs, face painting, and rituals involving symbols of power contained in a medicine bundle."

Today at the base of Chief Mountain one can find strips of bright-colored cloth tied to trees and brush, the remnants of offerings left by those on a modern day vision quest, by those who recognize their need to see in a new way.

Though the gospel writers would not have described the disciples of Jesus as people on a vision quest, in one way or another it seems that that is what they very well may have been. It is also what disciples still are, those with new eyes, longing to see the God who opened their eyes in the first place.

At heart believers are all vision questers of one sort or another. A more focused question might ask what sort of vision it is that we seek. I have come to think that most of us fall into one of two kinds of believers. There are those of us who seek to return to a better day. Present faith never seems to be as good as it once was. Young people used to know their religion and went to church. Parishes were better before neighborhoods changed. Priests and nuns once dressed like priests and nuns. Parishes never had to merge or close. In short, though they seem blind to the future and even to the present, these believers have no difficulty in seeing the past most clearly. For them, the vision quest is a journey into how it once was.

The other kind of believers are those of us for whom the better day is always in the future, to make the church into what it never yet has been. Present faith never seems as good as it could be: if only we had a married clergy; if women could be priests; if we used inclusive language; if we had a different pope. These believers see the future without shadows or clouds. Though blind to the goodness of the past and even of the present, the vision that drives them lies in how it could be.

There is, however, a third type of believer, of which there are only a few. We have come to call them saints. They are the ones who live in the moment of now, able to recognize the movement of God in human life as it brings a new kind of light. Like Samuel sent to find a new king and recognizing David to be the chosen one from among his brothers, they are able to recognize God's Spirit and where it dwells. And like the man born blind and given sight by Jesus, they live life with their eyes opened, not of their own doing but of God's doing. They do not look regretfully to the past or reproachfully to the future but awesomely to now. They refuse to be alert to anything but how God is unfolding in the present—not oblivious to what we once were or could be, but obvious to what we are in God already and cherishing it. They are the only ones who truly see; anything less is blindness.

*What is your vision? What do you seek? Do you know anyone who lives in the moment of now? What is it about them that makes them so? What keeps you from being like them?*

## ◝ Prayer • psalm 23

R. The Lord is my shepherd, there is nothing I shall want.

The Lord is my shepherd, I shall not want.
He makes me lie down in green pastures;
he leads me beside still waters;
he restores my soul. R.

He leads me in right paths for his name's sake.
Even though I walk through the darkest valley,
I fear no evil; for you are with me;
your rod and your staff they comfort me. R.

Surely goodness and mercy shall follow me
all the days of my life,
and I shall dwell in the house of the Lord
my whole life long. R.

# The Fourth Sunday (Year B)

2 Chronicles 36:14–17,19–23; Ephesians 2:4–10; John 3:14–21

*By grace you have been saved through faith, and this is not your own doing; it is the gift of God.*

A long time ago I clipped the following out of the newspaper, out of what was then the *Milwaukee Sentinel*. It's from a column by Alex Thien.

> At the age of 10, we think we can live forever. When we're 20, we think we can save the world. When the big 30 rolls around, we think we can save the company. When the 40th birthday arrives, we think we can save our children. Then, when we're 50, we think we can save our marriage. And by the time we're 60, we think we should save aluminum cans.

When I come upon this clipping in among all the clutter on top of my desk, it reminds me that given my own best efforts I really do not save much of anything. It is always God who does the saving and not me. I need to be reminded of that—even more often than once in a while.

I suppose we all are in need of such memory joggings, or Alex Thien would not have written the column. Maybe it is because we want to believe that we make a difference, or because we need to believe that someone is in control and if not God then at least we are, or maybe it is because we desperately want to redeem our flawed and dented selves. So for whatever reason we try saving everything in sight, hoping that at least one of our efforts will take root.

Robert Frost has his own way of telling the tale in his poem "The Death of the Hired Man." It is the story of Silas, a hired hand who always comes back when he is not needed, when there is no work to be done, and always leaves just when the haying season begins. This time he comes "home" for what seems to Mary, the farm wife, to be the last time. As Silas sleeps against the warmth of the kitchen stove, Mary waits on the front stoop for her husband, Warren. She cautions him to be kind to Silas for she suspects he has come home to die. And that is when Warren, dislodged by Silas' untimely returns, mockingly remarks, "Home is a place where, when you go there,/ They have to take you in." But Mary, in her wisdom, answers back, "I should have called it/ Something you somehow haven't to deserve."

68

It's a conversation rewound and replayed in our heads and in our struggles again and again. We find ourselves unwittingly thinking that if we do all the right things, when we die and go to heaven then God will have to take us in. If we say the right prayers and belong to the right religion and follow all the rules and believe all the right truths, then we will have earned salvation. Only then we will have saved ourselves and then there will have been no need for God's gracious goodness. Then we will have lifted ourselves up and not by the Lord Jesus. Then we will proclaim ourselves as the light to overcome darkness, and it will not be the death and resurrection of the Lord which does so.

Frost's Mary, of course, is the one who has it right—not just about Silas but about all of life as well. It is all something we somehow haven't to deserve—not the gift of light to see with some sort of faith, not the desire to live in some sort of goodness, not the grace to know there is a God who loves us, not the hope to trust, not the love to try and act justly. It is all something we somehow haven't to deserve.

Yet lo and behold we find all those gifts bouncing round and about in our lives, somehow even ricocheting off of our sin, and doing so in such a way that at some rare moments we even grow grateful for the ability just to save aluminum cans. At such moments even that becomes God's gift.

*Make two lists for yourself: one, those situations or people which you are inclined to think you have somehow saved over the course of life; and two, those aspects of your own life which have been saved from whatever without any doing on your own part. Reconsider the truth of the first list. Appreciate the graces of the second.*

## ⌒ Prayer • psalm 137

R. Let my tongue be silenced if I ever forget you.

By the rivers of Babylon
there we sat down and there we wept
when we remembered Zion.
On the willows there we hung up our harps. R.

If I forget you, O Jerusalem, let my right hand wither! R.
Let my tongue cling to the roof of my mouth,
if I do not remember you,
if I do not set Jerusalem above my highest joy. R.

# ·┌· The Fourth Sunday (Year C)

Joshua 5:9–12; 2 Corinthians 5:17–21; Luke 15:1–3, 11–32

*Let us eat and celebrate; for this son of mine was dead*
*and is alive again; he was lost and is found!*

Maybe the reason forgiveness is so very difficult for us is the fact that
we are not really sure what makes for forgiveness. Is it saying, "Oh,
that's okay. Forget it"? Is it pretending that what took place never really happened and so we just go on with life from there? Is it deciding
we will no longer feel hurt or rejected or ignored? Is it a willingness
to give in and do life the other person's way? Is it saying I will care for
you and do what is best for you no matter what?

This week's gospel suggests that forgiveness is about being a home
for someone who is returning. That is what the father in the story did;
he decided that when the time came, he would be a home for his
returning son. And as it turned out, he had to find a way as well to be
a home for the son who had never left. God offers a home to the people led through the desert by Joshua, and that is when they come to
understand God has forgiven them their sinfulness. That is when they
begin to see in a new way how they are God's chosen people.

Barry is one of the local street people who lives in and around the
parish where I work and live. He is pleasant and courteous and honest and wants to do things right, though he also struggles with his
own set of demons. For the most part Barry seems to be finding his
way through the mazes of life as each of us does in our own fashion.
In some ways, the people of the parish have become a family for
Barry, or at least a part of the family he has scattered about the neighborhood. Frequently, he will be gone for a time, and we will wonder
what happened to Barry only to find him drifting back among us.

These days Barry is angry with us. For whatever reason, the elderly
man he had been staying with and seemingly taking care of has let it
be known that Barry is no longer welcome. So Barry brought his
assembled belongings and took up residence on our garage roof. It is
a flat roof that has a two-foot-high wall about it, a place that affords
a bit of shelter from the wind. Soon, however, the parish came up
with an entire list of reasons why it would be best if Barry did not live
on our garage roof—safety, security, and insurance among them. So
Barry was asked to move on, and that's why Barry is angry with us.

The parish staff here tries to be sensitive and caring about the street people. They try to let them make their own way when that is what they want to do. Too often those in need don't want anyone to interfere, if for no other reason than to know there is something in their lives they can control for themselves. But the staff also does try to meet the needs of the street folk when those folk will allow them.

So here we are, wondering how to be a home for Barry while at the same time insisting he move on. If we play the role of the patient and welcoming father in the story, then we are confronted by the fact that we cannot always let people do what they want to do. We are reminded that there are such things as propriety and social custom. On the other hand, if we express some expectations, we find ourselves sounding much like the older son. Forgiveness and being a home for those who return becomes complicated and messy and confusing.

All of this is perhaps why we find forgiveness so difficult and why it may be that only God does it well. We just muddle along, not very sure about the process and seldom forgiving as well as we would like, just because we don't really know how to be a home for those who need one.

*What is your definition of forgiveness? Does the notion of forgiveness as being a home for someone make forgiveness more of a challenge or easier to offer?*

## ⌒ Prayer • psalm 34

R. Taste and see the goodness of the Lord.

I will bless the Lord at all times;
his praise shall continually be in my mouth.
My soul makes its boast in the Lord;
let the humble hear and be glad. R.

O magnify the Lord with me,
and let us exalt his name together.
I sought the Lord, and he answered me,
and delivered me from all my fears. R.

Look to him, and be radiant;
so your faces shall never be ashamed.
This poor soul cried, and was heard by the Lord,
and was saved from every trouble. R.

# ·↗· Monday, the Fourth Week

Isaiah 65:17–21; John 4:43–54

*Thus says the Lord: I am about to create new heavens and a new earth; the former things shall not be remembered or come to mind.*

There is in each of us a longing sewn into our spirit. It yearns to bring us to what we are meant to be. That longing is, in a way, an almost silent rumbling as if it were a primal rhythm of what is meant to be the human symphony. That yearning shows itself in many ways. We go through life desperately wanting our loves to nourish us, to overflow into sharing with another that which we treasure most. We want the work of our hands to bring forth beauty, and our celebrations to be gatherings of joy which renew all who join in. We want our children to outlive us, our dreams to be the pattern for a new creation, and our gardens to bear abundant fruit. We sense it is not enough to simply be alive. Unlike the rest the creation, we yearn for our longing to be filled. Or perhaps it is that we are simply so much more conscious of our yearning than the rest of creation seems to be.

Spiritual writers say that one of the signs of growing faith, of deepening holiness, is the trust that God is indeed making all things new. Some people feel we live in a world that at times seems to be collapsing in upon itself, like a black hole sucking in any and all fragments of light. Yet a person of faith stands in that same world in hope, in the profound trust that, in spite of it all, God is making life new. It is the person of faith who lives with inner peace, who looks without fear upon all that is. And, like the centurion who returned home in the trust that his son would be healed by Jesus, the person of faith does so as well, in part because the Lord has said he would. The person of faith has no reason to doubt. But it is also a vision which the person of faith brings to living, a vision not of what we see with our eyes, but of what we see with our faith, a vision of which the physical world is only a shadowed hint—true, but also easily misread.

The longing which gives hope to our everyday dreams is also the faith that enables us to trust without fear that all that is rests in God. It is the echo of resurrection woven into the fabric of human life. God does make all things new. God does bring all things to life. God does conquer death—even yours and mine.

*Do you consider yourself a person of deep faith? What is it that you see with your faith? Does your faith enable you to stand in hope in this world, even through seemingly dark times? Why or why not?*

## Prayer • psalm 30

R. I will praise you, Lord, for you have rescued me.

I will extol you, O Lord, for you have drawn me up,
and did not let my foes rejoice over me.
O Lord, you brought up my soul from Sheol,
restored me to life from among those gone down to the pit. R.

Sing praises to the Lord, O you his faithful ones,
and give thanks to his holy name.
For his anger is but for a moment;
his favor is for a lifetime.
Weeping may linger for the night,
but joy comes with the morning. R.

Hear, O Lord, and be gracious to me!
O Lord, be my helper!
You have turned my mourning into dancing.
O Lord my God, I will give thanks to you forever. R.

# ·/ᐟ· Tuesday, the Fourth Week

Ezekiel 47:1–9, 12; John 5:1–3, 5–16

*The angel brought me back to the entrance of the temple; there, the
water was flowing from below the threshold of the temple.*

Some time ago, Mrs. Lederman asked her class of fifth graders from
Story School in Milwaukee, "At what age would you want to drink
from the Fountain of Youth?" The thought of it all got their imagina-
tions flowing, probably not unlike the idea once did for Ponce de
Leon long ago. Wise Mrs. Lederman thought their dreams worth saving and sharing, and so she passed them on to the local newspaper,
the *Milwaukee Journal* (February 2, 1985). I saved the clipping, and
every once in a while I come across it, still tucked away in my desk
drawer. These were a couple of their fantasies.

> If I found the Fountain of Youth I would want to be sweet 16
> years of age. I would because all my friends are about 16. I could
> wear makeup. I could go out and stay out as long as I want. I
> could stay up until I fall asleep. That's why I want to be sweet
> 16. (Anne Marie)

> If I found the Fountain of Youth I would want to be 18 years of
> age because my sister is 18 and she can drive and she has a job
> at McDonald's. That's why I want to be 18. (Staci Marie)

> If I found the Fountain of Youth, I would want to be 30 years
> because then I would be just like a half an hour. I could have a
> girlfriend and get married so I wouldn't be lonely. (Steven)

The Fountain of Youth is supposed to have been a source of magical
water. We smile at the thought of it today and at Ponce's gullibility, if
indeed he bought the story. Yet we just as eagerly put out our own
hard earned resources for its modern versions—exercise machines
and body builders, facial creams and potions, hair dyes and cosmetic
surgeries. We modern folks have our own fountains of youthfulness,
many of them, and we are not hesitant to drink from them abun-
dantly.

Sooner or later, however, most of us come to admit (at least to ourselves) that not only do all such fountains fail to flow with youthfulness but also that we continue to grow flabby and old. In short, they
don't work, not any better than old Ponce's did some time long ago.

It is the person of faith, however, who also comes to discover that in so many ways it is the Lord Jesus who is the real fountain in our lives, not one of water, not one of youth, but one of life. He is the one who shows us how forgiveness frees us from the revenge that can cripple a life as much as arthritis can. He shows how love for others can be a great source of joy and energy, more than our teenage years ever were. His way of trusting is a strength that sustains well into a life already long with plentiful years.

So the one who drinks of the Lord Jesus through faith does indeed find life. Most of us, however, first drink freely of other fountains, and perhaps that is just the way we sort out what quenches our heavy thirsts and what does not. It would be nice if we all learned from those who have gone before us, but life seldom works that way. So in the meantime we all keep drinking of many fountains and pools and rivers, and sooner or later most of us come to the Lord Jesus who turns out to be the real life-giving water.

*How has the Lord Jesus been a fountain of life for you? What are some of the fountains you have tried over the course of your life-time? Are there any you are still drinking from?*

## Prayer • psalm 46

R. The mighty Lord is with us; the God of Jacob is our refuge.

God is our refuge and strength,
a very present help in trouble.
Therefore we will not fear, though the earth should change,
though the mountains shake in the heart of the sea. R.

There is a river whose streams make glad the city of God,
the holy habitation of the Most High.
God is in the midst of the city;
it shall not be moved;
God will help it when the morning dawns. R.

The Lord of hosts is with us;
the God of Jacob is our refuge.
Come, behold the works of the Lord;
see what awesome things he has brought on the earth. R.

# ◝ Wednesday, the Fourth Week

Isaiah 49:8–15; John 5:17–30

*The hour is coming, and is now here, when the dead will hear the voice of the Son of God, and those who hear will live.*

Some people thrive on challenges. They do better in a time crunch or when the task seems impossible or the resources are limited. They get a better grade on a twenty-page term paper if they do it the night before it's due to be handed in. They are more likely to get a job done if they have ten other things to do that day than if they have only one other thing to do. Conflict seems to feed productivity in them.

I cannot help but wonder if there is not something Godly about that aspect of human nature, if that is not a moment when we come face-to-face with God, or at least back-to-back or shadow-to-shadow. So often it seems that this is just when our God comes to the surface, when we are weighted in the darkness.

Think of it. Immerse a composer of music into the world of the deaf and you have a Beethoven. Put a creative genius into the cotton fields of slavery and you have an Eli Whitney. Trap a poetess in a shy and reclusive spirit and you have an Emily Dickinson. Put a passionate leader into a prison of apartheid and you have a Nelson Mandela. Imprison an artist in depression and you have a Van Gogh. Place a woman driven to justice into a nation of oppression and you have a Joan of Arc. Lower Joseph and his technicolor coat into a well and he saves the nation from famine. Cripple the Hebrews in a desert-locked exile, and they find a way home through the wasteland and back into a renewed promise. It is not a life of ease that seems to be the medium for God's love; rather, it is the struggles and limitations in which we find ourselves, as if God's passion for life cannot be suppressed.

More than anything, that seems to be what Jesus came not only to say but also to be—his Father's commitment to us, to be life even in the ultimate contradiction of death. And there are flickers of that all around us, when hardened hearts choose to forgive, when possibilities open up where we could not even imagine one, where healing finds a way, when disasters unite whether it be a marriage or a community, when love finally chooses us, when fertility blesses a barren womb, when opportunities knock, when death is able to be embraced because one believes in resurrection.

*Where have you found life when there had been only death? Do you live your life believing that God is committed to life? Recall a particular time when you lived out that conviction.*

## ʒ̃ Prayer • psalm 145

R. The Lord is kind and merciful.

The Lord is gracious and merciful,
slow to anger and abounding in steadfast love.
The Lord is good to all,
and his compassion is over all that he has made. R.

The Lord is faithful in all his words,
and gracious in all his deeds.
The Lord upholds all who are falling,
and raises up all who are bowed down. R.

The Lord is just in all his ways,
and kind in all his doings.
The Lord is near to all who call on him,
to all who call on him in truth. R.

# ↜ Thursday, the Fourth Week

Exodus 32:7–14; John 5:31–47

*The works that the Father has given me to complete, the very works*
*that I am doing, testify on my behalf that the Father has sent me.*

A friend of mine says that the spirit of poverty is living with the gifts
your friends and family give you for Christmas. Maybe. The reason I
smile whenever he says that is because I know it's so true. The fact is,
we do not like living with much of life as it is, whether that be on
December 26th or on any other day of the year. As it is we pick our
way through the bins of life, trying on and taking off, simply doing a
lot of exchanging as we go—or at least wishing we could.

I have often found myself thinking that if I left this or that parish
and went to another one, well, the new one just might not have all
the problems this one has. Married people find themselves wondering if this spouse was the right choice, and if maybe they should get
a divorce and start all over. Couples, too, will say to one another,
"Let's have one more child. We'll raise this one right." Employers
muse about whether they should renew someone's contract; maybe if
they hire someone else, just maybe, things will go more smoothly.
And on and on and on, we all think. We prefer to be able to exchange
life, and not just on December 26.

So there is something perhaps a bit redeeming to discover that the
same temptation has existed with God. God was inclined to sweep
the table clean of dirty dishes, and indeed did in Noah's time. And the
temptation arose again with Moses when the people took to wor-
shiping molten calves. So God was about to start all over once more,
the story says, except that this time Moses intervened and suggested
that God finish what God started, only Moses said it more kindly,
with more respect and more tact. And God stood corrected. God
sucked in the fiery breath he would have preferred to spew out and
agreed to finish what had been started. It seems the inclination to
want to start all over is a part of being a person, whether it be a
human one or a divine one.

Whatever it was that the people may have perceived God to be,
Jesus came to say that what God is for us today is faithfully present.
To those who doubted or fretted or argued, Jesus simply invited them
to listen to the testimony of John his cousin, or to the quality and
pointedness of what he himself was doing, or to the Scriptures them-

selves and what they say about God. In any case, Jesus would not back off. However the people may have considered God in the past, today God is known as faithfully present.

To this day believers have come to discover that truth—perhaps in the faithful love of one ever present, or perhaps in the reality of having been loved throughout life by family or friends or community. Or for some it may be in the gift of frequently coming to know God in prayer. Or in the fact that life has always come together, not necessarily without pain or struggle or confusion, but nevertheless eventually coming together as a whole. Or it may be in the blessings of life that continuously show themselves without our own efforts or plans. Wherever they may discover that truth, believers come to recognize a God not just present, but faithfully present. God no longer wants to exchange us for someone else.

*Name a sign of God's faithful presence which has been constant in your life. Have you ever considered starting anew in a particular aspect of your life? What was the reason for this desire? What did you do? Why?*

## ⌁ Prayer • psalm 106

R. Lord, remember us, for the love you bear your people.

Our ancestors made a calf at Horeb
and worshiped a cast image.
They exchanged the glory of God
for the image of an ox that eats grass. R.

They forgot God, their Savior,
who had done great things in Egypt,
wondrous works in the land of Ham,
and awesome deeds by the Red Sea. R.

Therefore God said he would destroy them
had not Moses, his chosen one,
stood in the breach before him,
to turn away his wrath from destroying them. R.

# ✶ Friday, the Fourth Week

Wisdom 2:1, 12–22; John 7:1–2, 10, 25–30

> *Let us lie in wait for the righteous man, because he is inconvenient*
> *to us; the very sight of him is a burden to us, because his manner of*
> *life is unlike that of others, and his ways are strange.*

Tom is a friend. He is also a salesman. He works for producers of
entertainment products—televisions and VCRs and boom boxes and
video cameras and all such sort. You get the idea. Well, Tom's job is
to get distributors to purchase large amounts of products which the
distributors then sell to retail stores. Tom is also honest, consistently
so, and this is where problems have begun to surface for him.

Tom's supervisors have been putting pressure on the sales staff to
move products. Not so unusual or surprising: that's their job. But part
of what they want the sales staff to do is to create urgency. In other
words, they want the sales staff to pressure the distributors into buy-
ing by saying there is a special purchase that has been obtained and
will only be available to the distributors for the next two days—which
Tom says is not true. It's all contrived, he explains. So Tom refuses to
lie, and his supervisors get angry and threatening, and that is when
the tension mounts.

As Tom explains it, the tension comes not only from the result-
ing fewer sales but also from the simple fact that he stands by his
principles, from the fact that goodness comes face to face with evil.
Tom doesn't use those words, but in effect that is what he says happens. I know Tom. I know he doesn't point fingers or call names. He
is not confrontational. He simply lives by goodness. Nothing more
is necessary.

All of us tend to look at ourselves in terms of our jobs and roles and
wonder how well we do. We wonder if we are good parents or teach-
ers or nurses or priests or whatever. Yet so often such wondering gets
translated into whether or not we are successful at whatever it is we do.
There is a difference, however, between success and goodness. Lent
brings us back to goodness, the sort of goodness Tom tries to live.

Success needs to produce. Goodness simply needs to be—nothing
more. Goodness bears fruit simply because it is there, because it is
present and recognized, and at times even when it is not recognized.
Goodness has its effect silently. Goodness makes the world new—
like Jesus.

*Name that goodness by which you live and by which you will not compromise. How has your goodness been tested? Has your instinct for goodness ever been compromised by a desire for success? If so, how did you react, and what did you do?*

## Prayer • psalm 34

R. The Lord is near to broken hearts.

The face of the Lord is against evildoers,
to cut off the remembrance of them from the earth.
When the righteous cry for help, the Lord hears,
and rescues them from all their troubles. R.

The Lord is near to the brokenhearted,
and saves the crushed in spirit.
Many are the afflictions of the righteous,
but the Lord rescues them from them all. R.

He keeps all their bones;
not one of them will be broken.
The Lord redeems the life of his servants;
none of those who take refuge in him
will be condemned. R.

# *⌐* Saturday, the Fourth Week

Jeremiah 11:18–20; John 7:40–53

> *When the people heard his words, some in the crowd said, "This is*
> *really the prophet." Others said, "This is the Messiah."*

I went for a winter hike the other day in a land preserve set aside by
the city. The preserve is a smorgasbord spread for all sorts of tastes—
some wooded areas now stripped down by winter to stark black and
white, some tall grass prairies eerily snow-blown, a lowland swamp
that croaks with frogs in mid-summer but now is frozen into silence,
some hills, too, and with them their mated valleys. There is a path, as
well, that threads them all like beads on a rosary, and on that day I was
making my way from one bead to another—praying my way, really.

It had snowed the day before, and now the path had become wind-
blown in places, alternating barren stretches with snow drifts. At one
such drift someone before me had written in the snow with big let-
ters, "It's time to take a stand." That was all. Nothing more. They had
not said a stand on what, whether for chocolate or vanilla, for the
Democrats or for the Republicans, for or against capital punishment.
The message simply said: "It's time to take a stand."

To take a stand and find oneself on the wrong side of an issue may
be troublesome; but the greater sadness, it seems to me, is to have
come to the end of one's life only to realize that one had never taken
a stand on anything of worth. And so most of us find ourselves taking a stand, usually on more than chocolate or vanilla. We choose a
political party, or perhaps we choose not to choose and remain an
independent. We take a stand on abortion and capital punishment,
on drugs and nuclear arms, on the poor and whether or not we as a
nation will care for them. And if we are believers we take a stand on
our God, or we are believers in name only.

Jeremiah took a stand on his God, and he found himself in the
midst of national rejection. Nicodemus took a stand on his God and
found himself in the midst of peer ridicule. Jesus took a stand on his
God and found himself standing in death. At some point in our faith
lives each of us comes to recognize that if our faith has not cost, then
it needs to be reexamined for its worth.

In Lent we do this most of all in light of the Lord Jesus, because we
have come to recognize that not to stand with him is ultimately not
to stand for anything of worth at all.

*In what aspects of life do you stand where Jesus stands? Are there aspects of life in which you do not stand where he does? in which you hedge or compromise?*

### Prayer • psalm 7

R. Lord, my God, I take shelter in you.

O Lord my God, in you I take refuge;
save me from all my pursuers, and deliver me,
or like a lion they will tear me apart;
they will drag me away, with no one to rescue me. R.

Judge me, O Lord, according to my righteousness
and according to the integrity that is in me.
O let the evil of the wicked come to an end,
but establish the righteous,
you who test the minds and hearts, O righteous God. R.

God is my shield,
who saves the upright in heart.
God is a righteous judge,
and a God who has indignation every day. R.

# The Fifth Week of Lent

# ⌒ The Fifth Sunday (Year A)

Ezekiel 37:12–14; Romans 8:8–11; John 11:1–45

*You shall know that I am the Lord, when I open your graves, and*
*bring you up from the your graves, O my people.*

"An old man, a young man, and life's greatest lesson," reads the cover
of *Tuesdays with Morrie*, Mitch Albom's chronicle of his visits with his
college mentor and professor who was slowly dying of ALS, Lou
Gehrig's disease. It is a sharing of Morrie Schwartz's wisdom as Albom
listens to it and molds it into a memoir of sorts.

The Morrie one comes to meet over the course of the book is someone in whom dying has birthed an abundance of life. In one sense it
was as if a dying man wanted to leave behind for others the truth he
had come to know and live. At another level, however, I wondered if
he would have come to realize it all had he not found himself slowly
dying. It was as if dying became a midwife to a lifelong pregnancy.

This last thought seems so confounding; that some mysterious
presence could still the groping violence of chaos in such a way that
deeper life can happen. *Tuesdays with Morrie* never named that mysterious presence, maybe never even recognized it. I would call it God,
and Jesus showed us its power. I would further like to suggest that
contemporary "chaos theory" has something to say about what was
taking place in Morrie Schwartz as he was dying.

In brief, chaos theory suggests that our experiences of chaos
should not be perceived as intrusions into the harmonious rhythms
of life, but rather as one of those very rhythms itself. As growth is the
movement from one way of knowing and living to another, a dis-
mantling needs to occur in order for a new way to come about. Thus
the chaos, a necessary piece of life not to be avoided but one to be recognized as a doorway into a new way of being.

Long before the advent of scientific theory, however, Jesus
enfleshed that same mysterious presence and with it confronted the
chaos of death. It has been passed on to us in the story of Lazarus, the
loved friend who died and was buried deep in death's power.

What happened in Lazarus was not his own doing but God's
doing. Nor is what happened in Morrie Schwartz his own doing. That
too, says the believer, was God's doing, as well as every other event
that finds life being called forth from the chaos of death. Dry bones
scattered in the desert are not necessarily limited to being a cemetery.

The call of God to the church to be a faithful disciple, then, does not come without its own chaos, without its own three days of tomb-life against the back of darkness. In fact, chaotic confusion seems to be a fifth mark of the church these days. Voices abound surrounding the issues of a consistent life ethic, the role of women in the church, a common ground for unity, inclusive language, the role of authority, questions regarding ordination. Such chaos, however, should not necessarily be misconstrued as cause for concern, for it may very well be the call of God taking us to a new and as yet unimagined way of being disciples.

For those called by the Lord to be disciples—Lazarus, his sisters Martha and Mary, the town folk who witnessed it all—their experience of chaos was not over. Eventually they would again find themselves trying to piece a call to glory together with suffering and crucifixion. Yet the call to follow tends to be disruptive of life, and not only once but with frequency. One cannot hear a call to fuller life unless one is willing to live in the home of death as well.

*Have you ever felt trapped in a kind of death? How were you freed from its power? What impact did it have on your faith? Name your own current chaos. Try to imagine where it might be calling you.*

╱╱•   **Prayer • psalm 130**

R. With the Lord there is mercy
and the fullness of redemption.

Out of the depths I cry to you, O Lord.
Lord, hear my voice!
Let your ears be attentive
to the voice of my supplications! R.

If you, O Lord, should mark iniquities,
Lord, who could stand?
But there is forgiveness with you,
so that you may be revered. R.

I wait for the Lord,
and in his word I hope;
my soul waits for the Lord
more than those who watch for the morning. R.

# ⌇ The Fifth Sunday (Year B)

Jeremiah 31:31–34; Hebrews 5:7–9; John 12:20–33

*Unless a grain of wheat falls into the earth and dies, it remains just a single grain; but if it dies, it bears much fruit.*

Dylan Thomas wrote the poem *Do Not Go Gentle Into That Good Night* for his agnostic father who was dying of throat cancer. In it he pleads with his father to fight the intruder, death. He begins with the words:

> Do not go gentle into that good night,
> Old age should burn and rave at close of day;
> Rage, rage against the dying of the light.

Dylan Thomas wanted his father to do battle with death, fiercely and relentlessly, daring to look the enemy in the eye and mocking that meddler with the spittle of defiance.

In stark contrast Jesus chose to walk deeper and deeper into death. He says to those who seek him out, "unless a grain of wheat falls into the earth and dies, it remains just a single grain." And again, "Whoever serves me must follow me." And yet once more, "And what should I say—Father, save me from this hour? No, it was for this reason that I have come to this hour." Jesus had a different law written upon his heart, a different law by which he lived and died.

In every age there are those rare souls who seem to be able to live by the spirit of Jesus and for whom bodily death is not the ultimate enemy. Like Jesus they are able to live by a different vision and walk a different path. Consider the words of Dr. Martin Luther King, Jr.:

> If a man happens to be thirty-six-years old, as I happen to be, and some great truth stands before the door of his life, some great opportunity to stand up for that which is right and that which is just, and he refuses to stand up because he wants to live a little longer...or he is afraid he will lose his job...he may go on and live until he's 80, and (then) the cessation of breathing in his life is merely the belated announcement of an earlier death of the spirit.
>
> Man dies when he refuses to stand up for that which is right. A man dies when he refuses to take a stand for that which is true. So we are going to stand up right here...letting the world know we are determined to be free.

It has been pointed out that one of the tasks of life is to learn how to die well. If we die a bit every day and with abundance on those days that may call for such, then at our final moment we will be able to stand before that specter face to face and not run, simply because we have met before and have been able to walk away the victor.

Dying well does not mean we do so without fear. Courage can blossom only at those times when we stand in a field of fear. Even the Lord Jesus "offered prayers and supplications with loud cries and tears to God," as the letter to the Hebrews takes pains to note. Dying well does not mean we do so cleanly. Dying is always an uprooting that disrupts and scatters everything nearby.

Nor does dying well mean we do so in control of the event. That is what is so devastating about death. It has complete and total control. At its best and at its worst the only way to die well is to say yes to it every time it demands our submission. And like the eye of stillness at the center of the hurricane, it is at the heart of death where we embrace resurrection and where the holy offers life. It is where we meet the Lord Jesus.

*Are you able to understand and accept death any better today than you once could? What have you learned about the art of dying?*

### Prayer • psalm 51

R. Create a clean heart in me, O God.

Have mercy on me, O God,
according to your steadfast love;
according to your abundant mercy
blot out my transgressions. R.

Create in me a clean heart, O God,
and put a new and right spirit within me.
Do not cast me away from your presence,
and do not take your holy spirit from me. R.

Restore to me the joy of your salvation,
and sustain in me a willing spirit.
Then I will teach transgressors your ways,
and sinners will return to you. R.

# ⌒ The Fifth Sunday (Year C)

Isaiah 43:16–21; Philippians 3:8–14; John 8:1–11

> *I am about to do a new thing; now it springs forth, do you not per-*
> *ceive it? I will make a way in the wilderness.*

I recently read that we humans are growing beyond the five senses and becoming multi-sensory beings, capable of experiencing more than the physical. Slowly, generation by generation, we are developing an awareness that there is more to life than simply the physical.

We listen to our intuition; we pay attention to our sixth sense; we discover a spiritual side to our personalities. Many people have mystical experiences, occurrences about which they hesitate to talk yet ones which are so real that those moments give direction to the rest of their lives. It is not about having visions or hearing voices, but it is about the deepest portion of oneself experiencing the center of life so profoundly that while words fail, conviction and faith do not.

William Irwin Thompson describes us five-sensory humans in this way. "We are like flies crawling across the ceiling of the Sistine Chapel. We cannot see what angels and gods lie underneath the threshold of our perceptions. We do not live in reality; we live in our paradigms, our habituated perceptions, our illusions we share through culture we call reality, but the true reality of our condition is invisible." Yet every once in a while we "flies" do catch a wink's gleam of the passion that sustains our existence.

If Isaiah's God did something new among the Israelites in distant exile, as this weekend's reading tells, it is that same God who is bringing us all to something new even today. Yet like Thompson's flies crawling upon the ceiling of the Sistine Chapel, most of the time we are too close to see much of what it is.

More than anyone it was Jesus who showed us most clearly what it is that our God is creating us into. Compassionate and just, generous and merciful, love in a wasteland of indifference. With him the desert flowed as it never had before.

So when we hear the story of Jesus forgiving the woman caught in adultery and of forgiving so unconditionally, of course we squirm. Most of us have not yet evolved to the point of being able to forgive very well, to forgive without any need to equalize the suffering. Maybe that is why we still like the idea of capital punishment and a kind of justice that balances scales pain for pain. Maybe it is because we are still in the process of becoming human with such a long way to go yet.

Something stirred in me when John Paul II forgave his would-be assassin. Something in me was movingly caught off guard when Terry Anderson said to media interviewers inquiring about his attitude toward his Beirut kidnappers, "I forgive them. Of course I do. I'm a Christian. I'm a Catholic. I have to forgive them." Something in me was proud about being human when those family members of Jeffrey Dahmer's victims who were able to forgive Jeffrey Dahmer did so publicly and openly.

God is indeed doing something new in us humans. St. Paul was so right when he wrote to the Philippians, "It is not that I have reached it yet, or have already finished my course; but I am racing to grasp the prize if possible, since I have been grasped by Christ Jesus. I do not think of myself as having reached the finish line...but push on to what is ahead."

*Do you tend toward justice or mercy when it comes to capital punishment and the purpose of our penal system? Have you ever experienced great mercy from someone? Spend some time remembering the moment.*

## ·⌒· Prayer • psalm 126

R. The Lord has done great things for us,
we are filled with joy.

When the Lord restored the fortunes of Zion,
we were like those who dream.
Then our mouth was filled with laughter,
and our tongue with shouts of joy. R.

Restore our fortunes, O Lord,
like the watercourses in the Negeb.
May those who sow in tears
reap with shouts of joy. R.

Those who go out weeping,
bearing the seed for sowing,
shall come home with shouts of joy,
carrying their sheaves. R.

# ☡ Monday, the Fifth Week

Daniel 13:1–9, 15–17, 19–30, 33–62; John 8:1–11

*Jesus straightened up and said to her, "Woman, where are they?*
*Has no one condemned you?" She said, "No one, sir." and Jesus*
*said,"Neither do I condemn you. Go on your way."*

The biblical stories of this day's gathering tell two tales, each of a
woman accused of committing adultery; one innocent yet treated as
if she were guilty, the other guilty yet treated as if she were innocent.
The first, Susanna; the second an unnamed woman found only in
John's gospel. Both were given a future by the workings of God's
Spirit.

To live without a future is maddening and a curse. There are those
who prefer death to life in prison, so devastating is the hopelessness
of a life robbed of any future. Others enter deep depression in the
face of life without love. Some choose suicide when life seems
drained of meaning. Others, humiliated by the public exposure of
their sin, withdraw into darkness never to be seen again in light. We
grow desperate when the bowl of our lives is cracked and everything
it holds drains into emptiness.

The God of our lenten journey promises a future to those of faith.
While it can be a future of justice for those trapped in injustice as
Susanna was, that future is not always one of balanced scales in this
lifetime. Certainly it was not such for the Lord Jesus who was himself
immersed in a death of injustice. Yet his future was found in that very
same death and became resurrection. For others, the future God
holds out may be one of mercy in the face of heavy sin. Our sin is
another shape to death, but it is also another way to experience an
unexpected future when God's forgiveness becomes a blessing.

Most of us at one time or another (and probably more than once
in our lifetime), find ourselves in need of a future. It is in finding ourselves being offered such a future that we also find ourselves in the
presence of God—when justice confronts injustice, when second love
springs forth from parched and hardened lives, when grave illness
succumbs to healing, when stony hearts crumble under the boon of
generosity, when mercy is offered for the seventy-seventh time
around. The God of our lenten days promises a future to people of
faith.

*If you live with a future at hand, name it for yourself, give thanks and recognize it as the gift of your God. If you long for a future, place it before your God in prayer. Ask for the grace of hope; seek peace.*

## Prayer • psalm 23

R. Though I walk in the valley of darkness,
I fear no evil, for you are with me.

The Lord is my shepherd, I shall not want.
he makes me lie down in green pastures;
he leads me beside still waters;
he restores my soul. R.

He leads me in right paths for his name's sake.
Even though I walk through the darkest valley, I fear no evil;
for you are with me;
your rod and your staff, they comfort me. R.

You prepare a table before me
in the presence of my enemies;
you anoint my head with oil;
my cup overflows. R.

Surely goodness and mercy shall follow me
all the days of my life,
and I shall dwell in the house of the Lord
my whole life long. R.

# ⟡ Tuesday, the Fifth Week

Numbers 21:4–9; John 8:21–30

*Jesus said to them, "Why do I speak to you at all? I have much*
*to say about you and much to condemn; but the one who sent me*
*is true, and I declare to the world what I have heard from him."*
*They did not understand.*

I'm not sure what the right world is, if there is a right one. I'm not
even sure what the real world is, and regarding the real world I know
there are a lot of candidates. Hard rock and rap, culinary delights,
cars, film, travel, gardening, and on and on. They are all somebody's
world; and because they come from God's hand, they are good.

The other day I was walking through a local mall and found myself
taking a short cut through Saks Fifth Avenue. They had on display a
nice-enough-looking shirt, and I casually looked at the price tag:
$185.00. I even looked at an identical shirt on the same rack just to
make sure the price was right. It was. That was not my world, though
it must be for some people.

Worlds can be confusing. I happen to like poetry, but I come across
a fair amount of poems in which I'm not quite sure what the poet is
trying to say. He or she obviously had some experience which
touched them deeply, but to me it seems to come from another
world. The same could be said for some films and for some musical
compositions and for some sculpture and paintings, as well. Art is
very much that way. What speaks of truth to one person does not
speak at all to another. So whose world is the real world?

Jesus spoke of worlds as well, and of belonging and not belonging.
He said to the Pharisees on one occasion, "You are from below, I am
from above; you are of this world, I am not of this world" (John
8:23). And so we are back to the question of worlds, of right ones and
wrong ones, of real ones and ones that seem not so real.

In many ways, the world Jesus came to take us into seems to be the
least real, and yet he consistently proclaimed it to be most real. Life
lived simply brings more joy than life with many possessions. Saving
oneself ends up being the road to losing oneself, and losing is the toll
paid on the road to being saved. Forgiveness unites and winning
divides. Love transforms human spirits, and power hardens them.
Service is the real form of leadership. And of course the ultimate contradiction—that one enters into life fully by dying totally, that life

does not end in death but that death ends in life.

Anyone at all reflective about their living eventually makes their way into the world Jesus revealed. Bit by bit we come to recognize his way as most real, only we come to recognize it slowly (as in over the course of a lifetime). It is a journey everyone makes—believer and non-believer alike. It is the world everyone eventually finds themselves living in, more or less, because ultimately it is the only world. The difference between the one who believes and the one who does not is the difference between having a map and finding one's way by trial and error.

*Describe your real world. What sorts of words do you find yourself using to do so? Which objects? relationships? poetic images? status? nature and creation? art?*

## Prayer • psalm 102

R. O Lord, hear my prayer; and let my cry come to you.

Hear my prayer, O Lord;
let my cry come to you.
Do not hide your face from me
in the day of my distress.
Incline your ear to me;
answer me speedily in the day when I call. R.

The nations will fear the name of the Lord,
and all the kings of the earth your glory.
For the Lord will build up Zion;
he will appear in his glory.
He will regard the prayer of the destitute,
and will not despise their prayer. R.

Let this be recorded for a generation to come,
that a people yet unborn may praise the Lord:
that he looked down from his holy height,
from heaven the Lord looked at the earth,
to hear the groans of the prisoners,
to set free those who were doomed to die. R.

# ⟡ Wednesday, the Fifth Week
Daniel 3:14–20, 91–92, 95; John 8:31–42

*Jesus said to the Jews who had believed in him, "If you continue in my word, you are truly my disciples; and you will know the truth, and the truth will make you free."*

I wish I were free. I would not have to be totally free as Jesus was in confronting the leadership of his day; just partially free would be okay. Free enough to be the sort of person I would like to be without distractions and hang-ups and fears and all such widgets I tend to collect. Free enough to do what I want to do, and free enough to be able to not do what I don't want to do, as the apostle Paul once put it. That's what is so appealing about the story of Shadrach, Meshach, and Abednego. They were free. They were able to stand up to King Nebuchadnezzar and the threat of his super-torched bonfire, and so not compromise their own faith. And they did it without flinching. If I could be half that free, I would be satisfied.

A few years back I decided I would give up potato chips for Lent, not because I believe God wants me to live on a potato chip-free diet, or because I think God likes to see me squirm in my addiction. No, I just gave up potato chips that Lent because I thought it might be a way for me to begin being in touch with what really controls me, a way of reminding myself that life should not be lived by every whim and desire. So I began fasting from potato chips. Well, I quickly came to realize that I was indeed helplessly hooked on those thinly-sliced, deep-fried, salty tubers, and with this insight came a wonder about what else there must be in my life which so weighs my spirit. If, indeed, something as simple as potato chips, then no doubt other passions as well.

That's one of the graces of Lent. The season brings us face-to-face with what enslaves us, not that potato chips are any big thing: they aren't. But being enslaved is. And part of what Lent is about for all of us is allowing the Lord Jesus to do his freeing thing in us, allowing him to confront us and offer us a different vision, maybe even bringing us to a different way of living.

On the other hand, we tend to like our enslavements. That is why they are there. They provide a comfort zone for us, whether it's our daily fix of potato chips or the afternoon soaps or sports or pop music, or whether it's a more notable element in our life, like control over the lives of family members or an indulgent salary. One way or another, each of us has chosen to live less free and that always keeps us from being who we could be. It is a trade-off of sorts.

In the end, freedom is not so much doing what you or I want to do or not do. It is much more becoming the sort of people we could be, not just because we put our mind to it, but even more so because we let the Lord Jesus take us wherever it is he lives. In that sense freedom is living without control simply because we live in the Lord.

*Is this lenten journey freeing you? emptying you? making you new? What is the connection, if any, between your answers to these questions and your lenten practice?*

## Prayer • Daniel 3

R. Glory and praise for ever!

Blessed are you, O Lord, God of our ancestors
and blessed is your glorious and holy name. R.

Blessed are you in the temple of your holy glory,
and to be extolled and highly glorified forever. R.

Blessed are you on the throne of your kingdom,
and to be extolled and highly exalted forever. R.

Blessed are you who look into the depths
from your throne on the cherubim. R.

Blessed are you in the firmament of heaven,
to be sung and glorified forever. R.

# ·⌐· Thursday, the Fifth Week

Genesis 17:3–9; John 8:51–59

*Jesus answered, "If I glorify myself, my glory is nothing. It is my Father who glorifies me, he of whom you say, 'He is our God.'"*

Faithfulness is a scarce commodity. Personnel contracts seem to be easily broken. Legislatures and politicians configure backroom deals. Love grows fickle. Friendships wane. The church does not always live the gospel it proclaims. There are even years when the season of spring seems to pass us by. Is anything in life faithful to the journey?

Into such lifelong abstinence comes a faithful God—not only as promise but as fulfillment, not only as Abraham's blessing of a host of nations but also as Jesus, the ever-human "I am." Despite the lyrics from Bette Midler's song, that God is watching from a distance, the melody God plays upon our lives is one of ever faithful presence, committed to being eternally human.

Show me, we all protest! And God says, "Look! I am here": in the experience of undeserved gentleness; in forgiveness sprouting from a crippled spirit; in amazing generosity that overflows all expectation; in the hope which refuses to wither among oppression and injustice; in the wonder of unexpected beauty; in God-with-us prayer which surprises us with its power; in the rhythms of life which bring forth more than we ask or even imagine; in self-sacrificing courage. And yes, when love is faithful and even embraces our unfaithfulness.

A lot of objections find their way to such a list: it's only a coincidence...the rhythm of life...human goodness coming to the surface...reading God into what already is. But of course, how else does the divine Spirit work in human life? Unexpectedly, unexplainably, and always but a shadow of the faithfulness we have come to know in Jesus, the one who is the Christ.

*How has God been faithful to you? Where have you experienced God's faithfulness? Draft your own list of divine faithfulness.*

## Prayer • psalm 105

R. The Lord remembers his covenant forever.

Seek the Lord and his strength;
seek his presence continually.
Remember the wonderful works he has done,
his miracles, and the judgments he uttered. R.

O offspring of his servant Abraham,
children of Jacob, his chosen one
he is the Lord our God;
his judgments are in all the earth. R.

He is mindful of his covenant forever,
of the word that he commanded for a thousand generations,
the covenant that he made with Abraham,
his sworn promise to Isaac. R.

# ⟋ Friday, the Fifth Week

Jeremiah 20:10–13; John 10:31–42

> *Jesus answered: "If I am not doing the works of my Father, then do not believe me. But if I do them, even though you do not believe me, believe the works, so that you may know and understand; that the Father is in me and I am in the Father."*

We all have a sense that our lives fall short of what we hope they would be, and all of us recognize the truth of "Actions speak louder than words." So in exasperation over the contradictions we live, we resort to "Do as I say and not as I do." It is always a moment of bold honesty for us—the realization and the confession that at times there is more wisdom in the words we speak than in the lives we live. Yet that confession is always declared with the added realization that such advice probably will not make a lot of difference. The receiving end of such homey wisdom is ultimately shaped more by our actions. Grudgingly, we realize that as well.

Curiously, the tensions and growing animosity in Jesus' life were precipitated between those who heard what his life was about in the works he did (the people) and those who heard his words but somehow missed his life (the leadership of his day). Try as he might to get them to see, or rather to hear, what his life was saying, the pharisees and the scribes latched on to the words from his lips and missed the words from his love. The ordinary folk seemed to have been able to read it all, and so became believers.

A while back I participated in a poetry writing workshop. One of the exercises was to create a poem by imitating the pattern of an accomplished poet. In other words, if the poet wrote a piece on death, we might choose to write ours on life, or on ice cream sundaes or planting a garden or spring rains. It didn't matter. What did matter, however, was that we were to mimic the poet. Wherever the poet used a noun, we were to use a noun. Wherever the poet employed a verb or an adjective, so were we. Phrases were to refer back to the same referent, and structure and rhyme were to mime that of the original. Subject and words were to flow from our own imagination. The pattern was to be that of the master poet. It was a good exercise. The intent was that over time we would take on the skills and instincts and wisdoms and abilities of the artist. We become what we imitate.

This is what Lent is about as well, or what you and I try to make it be about: imitating more closely the life and love of Jesus. And we do so with the faint hope that in the process we might indeed become a bit more like the artist, a bit more like the master, the holy one. So in Lent we pay added attention to forgiveness and service and generosity and surrendering our own petrified wills. Lent is about imitating the actions of the Lord Jesus with the thought that perhaps this year we may find ourselves saying "Do as I say and not as I do" one time less than we said it last year.

*What has been your experience of Lent so far this year? In what ways have you taken on the image of the Lord Jesus? From your lenten practices, how is the pattern of your own life a bit more like that of the Lord Jesus?*

### ⸙ Prayer • psalm 18

R. In my distress I called upon the Lord,
and he heard my voice.

I love you, O Lord, my strength.
The Lord is my rock,
my fortress, and my deliverer. R.

My God, my rock in whom I take refuge, my shield,
and the source of my salvation, my stronghold.
I call upon the Lord, who is worthy to be praised,
so I shall be saved from my enemies. R.

The cords of death encompassed me;
the torrents of perdition assailed me;
the cords of Sheol entangled me;
the snares of death confronted me. R.

In my distress I called upon the Lord;
to my God I cried for help.
From his temple he heard my voice,
and my cry to him reached his ears. R.

# ⟋⟍ Saturday, the Fifth Week

Ezekiel 37:21–28; John 11:45–57

*[Caiaphas] prophesied that Jesus was about to die for the nation,*
*and not for the nation only, but to gather into one the*
*dispersed children of God.*

If you catch me off guard in one of those moments when I am not defensive or self-conscious, you might get me to admit that I like boundaries. I am not sure this is a very good thing—liking boundaries—but I suspect it's true for most people. We tend to like boundaries; at least we tend to like the ones we like.

I like my half of the garage so there is enough room for me to get in and out of the car, so I don't have to be overly cautious about backing out or driving in, and so I can have a little extra room to store my stuff. I like garage boundaries. I think they can be good things.

The other day I was on a plane in the middle seat of a three-seat row. I tend not to like the middle seat because there's not much extra room there. The outer seats seem to be just a bit freer, maybe because of the couple of extra inches near the window or those spilling over into the aisle. Next to me on that plane was a woman who was less than conscious of her seating boundaries—not a lot, mind you, and she was a very pleasant person—but the seat boundaries between her and me became a tad distorted. I just think boundaries can be good things.

The boundaries of my own room, for example—I like those too. I don't have to be perfect when I'm inside those boundaries. I can be whomever I want—within boundaries, of course. But I like my room. And I also like my Green Bay Packers football team which lives within the boundaries of Wisconsin—my state. They belong to me, I like to think, because they are in my state, within my boundaries.

The poet Robert Frost noticed that people like boundaries. They like fences and walls and gates. He wrote about that sort of thing in "Mending Wall." "Good fences make good neighbors," Frost's farmer friend kept telling him. But Frost wasn't so sure. "Before I built a wall I'd ask to know/ What I was walling in or walling out," he mused. Robert Frost had some hesitations about boundaries, about them being so good.

Jesus must have been like that—someone who longed to break down barriers, to unite and heal and overcome divisions. I think he came to show us how we all have the same Father, to highlight our commonality and to suggest that we do not need boundaries, at least not all of them or so many of them. Yet that got the folks of his day a bit nervous and unsettled. They wanted to keep their own national identity as much as I want to keep my own garage space or my Green Bay Packers. The people of his day wanted boundaries as much as I do.

Much to Jesus' dismay, we keep on setting up boundaries. We worry about who is in the church and who is out and how to get people from one side to the other. We have been known to use up a fair number of words over such things as excommunication and denominational identity and boundaries between truth and falsehood. And if anyone suggests such energies may be misplaced, there are enough of us around to insist upon the contrary—with passion, no less.

I think this Lent could be a good time for me to break down some boundaries, personal or otherwise—as long as I can keep my own garage space. Maybe it would be a good time for you too.

*Name some boundaries you hold sacred. Name one you would be willing to erase or at least blur.*

## ♪ Prayer • Jeremiah 31

R. The Lord will guard us,
like a shepherd guarding his flock.

Hear the word of the Lord, O nations,
and declare it in the coastlands far away;
say, "He who scattered Israel will gather him,
and will keep him as a shepherd a flock." R.

For the Lord has ransomed Jacob,
and has redeemed him from hands too strong for him.
They shall come and sing aloud on the height of Zion,
and they shall be radiant over the goodness of the Lord. R.

Then shall the young women rejoice in the dance,
and the young men and the old shall be merry.
I will turn their mourning into joy,
I will comfort them, and give them gladness for sorrow. R.

# Holy
## Week

# ·/⌒· Passion Sunday

Isaiah 50:4–7; Philippians 2:6–11
Year A: Matthew 21:1–11: Passion narrative, Matthew 26:14—27:66
Year B: Mark 11:1–10; Passion narrative, Mark 14:1—15:47
Year C: Luke 19:28–40; Passion narrative, Luke 22:14—23:56

*Let the same mind be in you that was in Christ Jesus, who, though*
*he was in the form of God did not regard equality with God as*
*something to be exploited, but emptied himself.*

We need dreamers. The rest of us tap into them. We borrow their
dreams and make them our own. And because dreamers tend to live
on the edge of where life is lived, what they envision usually seems a
tad unreal to us. So we temper their work, flatten them out in a way,
and rework them so they fit into what we have come to know as life.
That is how it seems to take place anyway.

From early on in life we begin collecting dreams for ourselves. We
dream about what we are going to be when we grow up, of being
famous and popular and wealthy. We dream of a magnificent home
and of a life-style that turns heads as well as lives. We carry about in
our portfolio of fantasies what love will look like, marriage and family and happily-ever-after living for every day that's yet to come.

Somewhere in the middle and muddle of it all, however, the wind
shifts and the flag begins to furl in the other direction. One by one,
we begin to let go of those dreams we have been hoarding. We look
at our bank account and the elusiveness of wealth replaces the dream.
Our home is indeed our castle, yet far from the Better Homes and
Gardens dream variety. Those with whom we share life, those we love
and call family, look little like the dream we once pictured. We look
in the mirror and find imagined beauty that has grown wrinkled or
gray or balding.

In time those we love move away and still others die. We find ourselves needing to exchange our home for health care, and our future
for memories. Finally one last dream remains, one out of all those we
once had gathered—the dream that we can live forever. It is then, in
death and after we have surrendered every dream we have ever drafted, after we have been totally emptied, it is only then that we are filled
by our God, for even God cannot fill what is already full.

Life does seem to have an emptying process despite our own best efforts to the contrary. Regardless of how desperately we cling to our dreams and all of the meager shapes they take, our lives do become emptied, of dreams and loves and successes, even of future possibilities. And in the process, if we are open to it, we do find out attitude becoming that of Christ Jesus.

In the midst of these most holy days, we find ourselves discovering that Jesus' journey was the same as ours—one of being emptied so that we might be filled by our God, filled with resurrection and life. For most of us, this is frightening. On the surface it seems so radical, so deadly. Maybe that is why we take all week long to tell the story of Jesus in whose shadow our own story unfolds. We come back again and again to tell the story in bits and pieces, because it is too much to absorb in one sitting, all the while knowing the ending. Yet it is in knowing the ending, one of resurrection, that we have the courage to even begin the telling.

*Has the emptying process for you yet begun? Which dreams have you already surrendered? Which dreams still hold a place front and center?*

## Prayer • psalm 22

R. My God, my God, why have you abandoned me?

All who see me mock at me;
they make mouths at me, they shake their heads;
"Commit your cause to the Lord; let him deliver,
let him rescue the one in whom he delights!" R.

For dogs are all around me;
a company of evildoers encircles me.
My hands and feet have shriveled;
I can count all my bones. R.

They divide my clothes among themselves,
and for my clothing they cast lots.
But you, O Lord, do not be far away!
O my help, come quickly to my aid! R.

# 🍂 Monday of Holy Week

Isaiah 42:1–7; John 12:1–11

*Mary took a pound of costly perfume made of pure nard, anointed Jesus' feet, and wiped them with her hair. Jesus said, "She bought it so that she might keep it for the day of my burial."*

A friend and I stopped in at a restaurant not long ago, just to get a bite to eat. It's an eastside sort of place, more of a coffee shop than anything else. Generally the folks who gather there are laidback and easygoing. We had ordered some coffee and were wrapped in conversation, when suddenly our waitress rushed by our table in tears and sobs and ran out into the kitchen. An elderly woman a few tables away was obviously dissatisfied with the service and made her displeasure known to our shared waitress—and to most of the others in hearing distance. Quickly other tableservers came to fill the gaps in service and to warm everyone's meal with attention. Later, our own waitress returned, a bit red-eyed but also a bit more courageous. She apologized to us for the ruffled service, though she needn't have, and then moved back into the calmed eye of the nearby table-storm.

It all brought home once more how service in one way or another is really a call to tears. It is so much more than filling water glasses and serving from the left and removing from the right and all such pleasantries. Service of almost any kind gets messy and ragged and shredded with the best of intentions. In some ways, it is a kinder form of slavery, but slavery nonetheless.

When the church tells the tale of Mary washing the feet of Jesus with perfume, it is not so far removed from Holy Thursday's tale of Jesus washing feet with water. The first, an early echo of looming death; the second, an awkward reminder of service to others, Jesus-style. Yet the two washings stand almost side-by-side within the same week, which perhaps makes them front and back sides of the same coin. Death and service—not two stories but one story.

So when we sometimes glibly talk about the call to serve, it is really also an invitation to do some dying, or maybe a lot of dying. The reality is that when we seek to free someone from anger, we do it by absorbing their anger, and that does something to us. When we seek to free anyone from their sin, we do so by embracing them with mercy, and in the process some of their sin may rub off on us. When we seek to free those enslaved in darkness, we do it by being the sort of light which enlightens by being consumed—a human form of candle power.

It all leaves us amassed in tension. On the one hand, what good are we if we suffer burnout? On the other hand, what sort of believers are we if we strenuously avoid getting tangled up in other people's lives, in other people's messes? Perhaps this is why we believers take an entire week to tell the story of suffering, death, and resurrection— because if we told it all in a day it would be too easy to slip out from under the tension of being called to suffering servanthood. So we take a week to tell the story, to live with the tension, to make sure it seeps into the cracks and crevices of our psyches. And what do we do with all of that tension? Well, perhaps the only thing we can do: live with it and die with it too, which is what Jesus did. And it may be that that is the good news of it all.

*In those times when you have chosen to be of service, are you able to recognize what it is that you have died to? what is becoming new life in you?*

### Prayer • psalm 27

R. The Lord is my light and my salvation.

The Lord is my light and my salvation;
whom shall I fear?
The Lord is the stronghold of my life:
of whom shall I be afraid? R.

When evildoers assail me
to devour my flesh—
my adversaries and foes—
they shall stumble and fall. R.

Though an army encamp against me,
my heart shall not fear;
though war rise up against me,
yet I will be confident. R.

I believe that I shall see the goodness of the Lord
in the land of the living.
Wait for the Lord; be strong,
and let your heart take courage; wait for the Lord! R.

# ⨍ Tuesday of Holy Week

Isaiah 49:1–6; John 13:21–33, 36–38

> *Little children, I am with you only a little longer. You will*
> *look for me; and as I said to the Jews so now I say to you,*
> *"Where I am going, you cannot come."*

Rudyard Kipling wrote a poem entitled "If"—perhaps to his son, perhaps to us all. It opens with these lines:

If you can keep your head when all about you
Are losing theirs and blaming it on you;
If you can trust yourself when all men doubt you,
But make allowance for their doubting too....

Yours is the Earth and everything that's in it,
And—which is more—you'll be a Man, my son!

In these days of Holy Week the poem also bears the image of Jesus. When life was collapsing about him and all were losing their heads, Jesus was the one who not only kept his head but kept his faith as well. When Judas slipped off because it was night and time to do what he was to do, when Peter was unknowingly inching his way into triple denial, when reading the signs of the times brought the knowledge of impending doom, Jesus was the one who stood faithful and committed. And because he did, we who try to live his story within our own lives find ourselves struggling to remain faithful and committed as well.

It is a struggle, however, to remain faithful and committed without losing our heads. It's a struggle when we stand alone in the midst of a collapsing life or a collapsing marriage, in the midst of blind illness or surrounded by deep death, in the midst of the confusion of midlife or the uncertainty of a jobless future. Whatever our collapse, we tell the story of Jesus' faithfulness in order to find courage for ourselves, and we do it because most of us do not stand alone very well.

Perhaps that is why we come together these days to tell the story of Jesus—so we do not have to stand alone. We stand together, because we believe that together he is with us. He becomes our courage and strength in ways we do not understand but in ways we also know are very real.

110

*When do you feel most alone? How do you bring your faith to such moments? What helps you stand faithful and committed in the midst of the ordinary and extraordinary events of your life?*

### Prayer • psalm 71

R. I will sing of your salvation.

In you, O Lord, I take refuge;
let me never be put to shame.
In your righteousness, deliver me and rescue me;
incline your ear to me and save me. R.

Be to me a rock of refuge,
a strong fortress, to save me,
for you are my rock and my fortress.
Rescue me, O my God, from the hand of the wicked. R.

For you, O Lord, are my hope,
my trust, O Lord, from my youth.
Upon you I have leaned from my birth;
it was you who took me from my mother's womb. R.

My mouth will tell of your righteous acts,
of your deeds of salvation all day long.
O God, from my youth you have taught me,
and I still proclaim your wondrous deeds. R.

# ·/⌒· Wednesday of Holy Week

Isaiah 50:4–9; Matthew 26:14–25

*Jesus took his place with the twelve; and while they were eating,*
*he said, "Truly I tell you, one of you will betray me."*
*And they became greatly distressed.*

Most studies of culture and life tell us what we already know; they simply confirm our suspicions and intuitions. But not always. Sometimes they crack the crystal of our stereotypes. Take personal violence, for example. What we have come to discover is that the victim in most instances has known the perpetrator. Murders are most frequently committed by family or friends, someone close to us. In the end, people find themselves betrayed by the very one with whom they have shared life's table.

In one way or another, I suppose, all of us have found ourselves playing out some scene of being betrayed. No doubt, more than once. A spouse's infidelity or abandoned desire to make a marriage work. A grown child's decision to build a wall of isolation with layers of bricked anger. A sibling who chooses to sever ties. The ache of a friend's remark. An employer's dismissal after years of service. All of us find ourselves betrayed by the very ones with whom we have shared life's table.

It is at such moments that people of faith lean on the Lord, that we discover how "it is the Lord God who helps me," not in any way that reorders the world or life or our own personal stories according to our own desires, but in a way that simply allows us to lean on loving presence. It is also such moments that "the Lord God has given me the tongue of a teacher, that I may know how to sustain the weary with a word." And in the process we become wounded healers, able to free others from pain because we ourselves have made the same journey.

*Are you a wounded healer? Name a recent time when you brought*
*healing to someone because of your own wounds. How were you*
*affected by this service?*

### Prayer • psalm 69

R. Lord, in your great love, answer me.

It is for your sake that I have borne reproach,
that shame has covered my face.
I have become a stranger to my kindred,
an alien to my mother's children.
It is zeal for your house that has consumed me;
the insults of those who insult you have fallen on me. R.

Insults have broken my heart,
so that I am in despair.
I looked for pity, but there was none;
and for comforters, but I found none.
They gave me poison for food,
and for my thirst they gave me vinegar to drink. R.

I will praise the name of God with a song;
I will magnify him with thanksgiving.
Let the oppressed see it and be glad;
you who seek God, let your hearts revive.
For the Lord hears the needy,
and does not despise his own that are in bonds. R.

# ·⌒· Holy Thursday

Exodus 12:1-8, 11-14; 1 Corinthians 11:23-26; John 13:1-15

*Then he poured water into a basin and began to wash the disciples'
feet and to wipe them with the towel that was tied around him.*

"The least we can do is eat together," is what my mother would say.
And so it was. As in any home and every family, in ours there were
ups and downs, times when we got along and times when we chose
a steeled and frozen silence. Sometimes we fought and sometimes we
loved which, as I think about it now, included the fighting as well as
the kindnesses. But always my mother would insist, "The least we can
do is eat together."

I know in some families when anyone was particularly uncooper-
ative or difficult to live with, the practice was to send them to their
room without supper. I know because that was how it was with my
friends. But that was not how it was at our house. In our family everyone always had to come to the table for meals, no matter how obnox-
ious we had been, no matter how disagreeable. The least we could do
was eat together.

Eating together and loving together: it can be a chicken-or-the-egg
sort of thing. Which comes first? Do we eat together because we have
loved one another and cared about one another and been there for
one another? Or do we love one another because we have eaten
together? As always, the answer is "yes." In our house, however, it was
the eating together which came first, which moved us to eventually
treat one another as brothers and sisters. Indeed, I grew up thinking
that if we could not at least eat together then we would never really
love one another.

When we gather together as believers it is taken for granted that
because we have eaten together we will also in some way or another
be loving one another. This is presumed, and rightly so. That is what
it is all about. Tonight, however, is different. We offer loving service
by washing feet, and we share a meal together. On this night we invert
the order. We do the loving first, as if to say the least we can do is love
one another. After that we share a meal, and then we go out to die.

Tonight we let a terrible secret out of the bag, that the eating
together is not just about loving one another but also about dying for
one another. Maybe that is why we only do both once a year and why
it is only during this week, because we are able to live with the dying

part only when we also tell the rising part. Otherwise it might be more than any of us are able to bear.

It may also be why in some families at mealtime the disagreeable ones are dismissed from the table to their rooms, simply because no one is in the mood to do any loving of them much less any dying for them. On the other hand, that very fact seems to be all the more reason for at least eating together, which then brings us full circle to where we began.

It isn't much of a meal that seals such a commitment. Some would refer to it only as a token. No matter. It is enough, at least it was for Jesus on the night before he died. In fact, so powerful and so memorable was that token meal that disciples have been doing the same ever since.

*To what extent are sharing a meal and commitment to one another interrelated for you? Has sharing a meal with someone ever changed your relationship to that person? when? with whom?*

## Prayer • psalm 116

R. Into your hand I commit my spirit.

What shall I return to the Lord
for all his bounty to me?
I will lift up the cup of salvation
and call on the name of the Lord. R.

Precious in the sight of the Lord
is the death of his faithful ones.
O Lord, I am your servant;
I am your servant, the child of your serving girl.
You have loosed my bonds. R.

I will offer to you a thanksgiving sacrifice
and call on the name of the Lord.
I will pay my vows to the Lord
in the presence of all his people. R.

# ·/⌒· Good Friday

Isaiah 52:13—53:12; Hebrews 4:14–16; 5:7–9; John 18:1—19:42

> *He was oppressed, and he was afflicted, yet he did not open his mouth; like a lamb that is led to the slaughter, and like a sheep that before its shearers is silent, so he did not open his mouth.*

I sometimes wonder if Jesus ever second-guessed himself, questioning his decisions or wishing he had kept his mouth shut even if he was right. Or did he simply decide to proceed forward without even a glance in hindsight to what might have been? like a seedling committed to the sun? or a hawk to the kill once it has spotted its prey? Then there is nothing to dissuade or distract. Is that what happened when his cousin John was beheaded, that he came to see what needed to be said and done and so he moved with it, plainly and without hesitation? Was he blinded by his passion so that he became a little bit crazy, unable to stop it all when that is what seemed called for to everyone else?

A friend called the other day. We hadn't talked in months, and so it was one of those phone calls that gathers up all the happenings scattered over the recent past, a hodge–podge quilt of sorts to keep the friendship warm. Early in the conversation, just after we had said hello and how are you, she asked what my passion was these days. What was I eager about and driven by? It caught me a bit off guard, only because I had not been thinking about it. As I recall I hemmed and hawed and stuttered something about life in the parish. It didn't seem right to say I didn't know, even if I really did not know. At the moment it seemed I should have a passion.

Much later in the conversation, she said something about her daughter's advice to her that she should find a passion—something which would ease the day-to-day strains between the two of them. (Oh, that's where that question came from, I thought.) "So, I'm thinking of taking a course in photography," she said. "I think I'd like that."

After we had said our good-byes, I thought about it all, and about having a passion. I realized then that we cannot choose a passion only because passions choose us and not the other way around. But I had not thought of that while on the phone, so it never got to be said.

Passions drive us. And if they are worthwhile, if they come from God as did those in the life of Jesus, then we stand in quiet courage upon committed lives, driven to goodness by some preordained call.

Passion happens. To Nelson Mandela, imprisoned as if in transparent amber by the unrelenting truth of his convictions. To a lone and anonymous student remembered forever because he stood in defiance of the military in Tianamen Square. To Mary, the mother of Jesus, who uttered the craziest of all yeses that set her life spinning out of any control except by that of her God. To say nothing of teenagers daring to choose uncommon mores among their peers, and heads of households working in jobs without satisfaction in order to nurture their family, and elderly people reluctantly raising yet a second family of their children's children. Passionate commitments happen.

These days we find ourselves telling the story of Jesus, or at least the ending of his story. It is the story of someone who fully entered into life, was passionately committed to it and also messed up by it, was seldom treated fairly by it, and then was robbed of it, even wondering in the midst of it if his Father was still there with him. And in the end it all collapsed. According to John's gospel, at that point resurrection happened. And that is how it is with passion.

*What in your life are you passionately committed to? How and when did you discover your passion? Where have you found goodness in the rhythms of your life?*

## Prayer • psalm 31

R. Father, I put my life in your hands.

In you, O Lord, I seek refuge;
do not let me ever be put to shame;
in your righteousness deliver me.
Into your hand I commit my spirit.
you have redeemed me, O Lord, faithful God. R.

I am the scorn of all my adversaries,
an object of dread to my acquaintances;
those who see me in the street flee from me.
I have passed out of mind like one who is dead;
I have become like a broken vessel. R.

But I trust in you, O Lord;
I say, "You are my God."
My times are in your hand;
deliver me from the hand of my enemies and persecutors. R.

# ⌒ Easter Vigil

Genesis 1—2:2; Genesis 22:1–18; Exodus 14:15—15:1; Isaiah 54:5–14;
Isaiah 55:1–11; Baruch 3:9–15, 32—4:4; Ezekiel 36:16–28; Romans
6:3–11; Matthew 28:1–10 (Year A); Mark 16:1–8 (Year A);
Luke 24:1–12 (Year C)

> *The angel said to the women, "Do not be afraid; come, see the place*
> *where he lay. Then go quickly and tell his disciples."*

Faith can have the look of high dives and bicycles without training
wheels and life without one's "blankey" and all such other momen-
tous confrontations with the specter of death. From youth on our
lives seem to be laced with the loss of control, and unless we embrace
such moments not only will we never really grow up, but neither will
we ever become people of faith who live in the resurrection.

One morning around eight o'clock I stopped in at a neighborhood
coffee shop, partly for a cup of coffee and partly just to watch the
folks. A mom came in with her five-year-old and took the table next
to my booth. I sort of couldn't help but overhear.

*Child:* Mom, I wouldn't have to go to school today. I could stay
home with you.

*Mom:* I know you could, Joe, but I think Mrs. Burns would miss
you.

*Child:* But won't you miss me, mom?

*Mom:* Sure, Joe, but I know you'll be back in the afternoon, and
I can be with you then.

*Child:* But I could help you in the kitchen.

*Mom:* What do you think you'll be doing in school today? It's
getting close to Easter, and I bet Mrs. Burns will probably be
having you make bunnies.

*Child:* Yeah, maybe. Mom, I think my tummy hurts.

*Mom:* Oh, I think it'll probably get better once you get to school
and are busy doing things.

*Child:* Mom, couldn't I stay home with you today? I'll miss you.

*Mom:* I know you will, Joe, but it's only for a couple of hours.
How's your apple juice?

*Child:* Okay. Mom, I think it would be okay if I stayed home
today.

And so the conversation continued. By the time they left, little had changed. It looked as if Joe was going to school.

Joe's mom was teaching Joe a number of things that day. Obviously, that school and learning are important. Also, that there are portions of life from which we cannot back away, and that satisfaction at times must be postponed. It was not the first time, I am sure, that Joe had to come to terms with those lessons, or the last.

There was a faith lesson unfolding as well for Joe, though I really do not know whether Joe and his mom were believers of any sort. At one level, however, it did not matter much. The groundwork was being laid. To become a believer, one has to come to terms with death and discover the life that lurks even there, waiting to be found. Joe was inching his way in.

Over the years I have grown in the conviction that the only way to become a believer in the resurrection is to walk into the tomb yourself and there discover that where you thought death lived, in reality now there is only life. To come to believe in the resurrection by any other way is to hold to someone else's belief and not to have your own. Joe's mom was teaching Joe how to walk into the tomb. That is the beginning of faith in the resurrection.

Joe is not the first one who has had to take that step. Nor is his mom. Nor you or I. The Easter gospels tell the tale of the first time. They are about the women who had become disciples, and they are about Peter and the other apostles. All of them, on their own various journeys, arrive at the tomb but do not go in. It is the home of death, and all of us would prefer not to visit that dwelling place. Only at the angel's invitation do the women go in and see for themselves. And Peter, he goes into the tomb and finds all of death's leftovers (like wrappings and cloths) but no death. That is when all of them become believers—after they have entered the home of death and discover it to be abandoned.

That is the pattern of coming to faith in the resurrection. We have to enter the place of death before we can come to discover it is no longer the force we once thought it was. It wasn't enough for Peter to have been told of the resurrection by Mary Magdalene. He had to discover it for himself, or he would never have really believed.

Discovering faith begins with moments that do not have the look of faith at all, like when we are standing at the end of a diving board or giving over the security blanket of our lives or daring some new venture or taking a long and risky look at ourselves. Such moments may not yet be faith, but they are the first wobbly steps into empty tombs that echo with the cry: Alleluia!

*When was the last time you consciously chose a course of action that seemed to be taking you into a tomb of sorts? What came of your choice? Is your faith based upon your own experience of death into life or do you believe because someone else has told you it is true?*

## ⟡ Prayer • psalm 118

R. This is the day that the Lord has made;
let us rejoice and be glad in it.

O give thanks to the Lord, for he is good;
his steadfast love endures forever!
Let Israel say,
"His steadfast love endures forever." R.

The right hand of the Lord is exalted;
the right hand of the Lord does valiantly.
I shall not die, but I shall live,
and recount the deeds of the Lord. R.

The stone that the builders rejected
has become the chief cornerstone.
This is the Lord's doing;
it is marvelous in our eyes.R.